At Issue

Reproductive Rights

Other Books in the At Issue Series

At Issue

| Reproductive Rights

Anne Cunningham, Book Editor

GREENHAVEN
PUBLISHING

Published in 2018 by Greenhaven Publishing, LLC
353 3rd Avenue, Suite 255, New York, NY 10010

Articles in Greenhaven Publishing anthologies are often edited for length to meet page
requirements. In addition, original titles of these works are changed to clearly present
the main thesis and to explicitly indicate the author's opinion. Every effort is made to
ensure that Greenhaven Publishing accurately reflects the original intent of the authors.
Every effort has been made to trace the owners of the copyrighted material.

Cover image: Suz7/Shutterstock.com

Library of Congress Cataloging-in-Publication Data

Names: Cunningham, Anne C., editor.
Title: Reproductive rights / Anne Cunningham, book editor.
Description: New York : Greenhaven Publishing, 2018. | Series: At issue |
  Includes bibliographical references and index. | Audience: Grades 9 to 12.
Identifiers: LCCN 2017039269| ISBN 9781534502062 (library bound) | ISBN
  9781534502093 (pbk.)
Subjects: LCSH: Reproductive rights—United States—Juvenile literature.
Classification: LCC HQ766.5.U5 R475 2018 | DDC 613.9—dc23
LC record available at https://lccn.loc.gov/2017039269

Manufactured in the United States of America

Website: http://greenhavenpublishing.com

Contents

Introduction

The term "reproductive rights" encompasses far more than a woman's constitutionally protected right to terminate an unwanted pregnancy. Access to accurate, age appropriate sex education, affordable contraception, and essential heath services such as prenatal care, breast cancer screenings, and even mental health counseling all fall under the heading of reproductive rights.

Despite a statement by the World Health Organization recommending that individual decisions about reproduction be free of violence or coercion, this is rarely the case worldwide. Even in the United States, a wealthy and developed nation, access to quality reproductive health care services is shrinking. Availability of these services has always varied widely according to income, race, and geographic location, but new legislation threatens to widen these existing disparities in access. It is more important than ever to reiterate that reproductive rights are fundamental human rights, rights to which we are all entitled in theory but must struggle to actualize in practice.

The claim "reproductive rights are human rights" may not strike us as controversial, but reproductive rights are among the most bitterly fraught social issues in contemporary politics. A glance at the news underscores that reproductive rights are under the gun, primarily from lawmakers who wish to curtail them based on religious or ideological grounds. Advocates for reproductive rights counter that a conservative minority should not dictate law and public health policy, nor should they interfere in private decisions made between a woman and a doctor. From both economic and public health standpoints, multiple studies suggest we have much to lose by rolling back reproductive rights.

The main reason reproductive rights are so contentious can be summed up in a single word: abortion. "Anti-choice" abortion opponents feel strongly that a human life begins at conception and that the termination of an embryo is tantamount to murder. While an answer to this thorny philosophical question of when life begins lies outside the scope of this book, the zeal and certainty with which abortion opponents answer this question ensures that legislation and court decisions concerning abortion will be passionate—and sometimes lethal. For example, in 2009, a Kansas doctor named George Tiller, known to perform abortions, was shot and killed while attending church. While only a few extremists resort to murder, anti-choice politicians justify their violent obstructions of women's reproductive rights by invoking a false equivalence of violence against the unborn child.

Anti-choice leaders are willing to sacrifice a bevy of reproductive rights because they believe these actions will reduce abortions. But is this conclusion correct? The central irony of their position, as a few of the viewpoints here will convincingly argue, is that the most effective way to prevent abortion is through inexpensive, readily available birth control and a sex education curriculum that moves beyond an "abstinence only" approach. With a few exceptions, the Affordable Care Act (ACA) requires insurers to cover contraception. Since this became law, the incidence of abortion in America has declined. Nonetheless, defunding Planned Parenthood and abstinence-only sex education remain high priorities for many Republican politicians.

How did we arrive in a climate so hostile to abortion and reproductive rights? Back in 1973, the Supreme Court upheld a woman's constitutional right to a legal abortion with their decision in the landmark case *Roe v. Wade*. The court hedged this protection by specifying that the state play a role in protecting the health of the mother and the potential life of the child. This caveat allows states considerable leeway to define conditions under which abortion is illegal, as well as other specifics regarding the procedure. On the federal level, pushback against *Roe* began almost immediately. In 1976, the Hyde Amendment prohibited any federal funds from being used for abortion. This is the pretext under which the movement to defund Planned Parenthood operates. As Bridgette

Dunlap explains in her viewpoint here, attacks on abortion "are on its availability and affordability, not its legality."

The 2010 midterm election also represented a significant turning point for abortion rights. That year, a spate of Republican politicians hostile to abortion rights gained power on both the state and federal level. Literally hundreds of new restrictions on the procedure have been passed in state legislatures since. Tactics include targeted regulation of abortion providers (TRAP) laws designed to shut down abortion clinics through onerous codes, enforced waiting periods, and requirements to counsel women from scripts often containing misinformation. Many of these laws, such as Texas HB2, have been struck down as unconstitutional due to their gratuitous and excessively burdensome nature.

Of course, the Republican presidential victory in the 2016 election promises to exacerbate the backlash. While President Donald Trump's personal views on abortion are inchoate and hardly consistent, his running mate and now vice president Mike Pence has been one of the most ardent foes of reproductive rights on the political scene for decades. One of Trump's first executive actions was to reinstate the so-called Global Gag Rule, which forbids funding for any NGOs to provide abortion or abortion related services. This reverses Obama's policy and cuts aid to the most needy.

Those who oppose such policies are numerous, and on January 21, 2017, they made their voices heard. The Women's March on Washington drew 500,000 to the nation's capital, and 3 million worldwide participated. Still, problems of unity and inclusiveness threaten to divide the resistance, as Karen Grigsby Bates points out in her viewpoint here. As a strong and united defense of reproductive rights is crucial, these critiques are instructive in building effective resistance.

This At Issue volume comprises articles that trace this debate. It aims to provide a nuanced and critical look at a subject that at some point will affect all of us. If we wish to expand reproductive rights in this country, we must begin from an informed and historically grounded position. This book seeks to foster this crucial knowledge.

1

State Legislatures Hammer Away at Abortion Access

Center for Reproductive Rights

The Center for Reproductive Rights (CRR) is a global legal advocacy organization that seeks to advance reproductive rights. The organization's stated mission is to "use the law to advance reproductive freedom as a fundamental human right that all governments are legally obligated to protect, respect, and fulfill."

The year 2010 marked an extremely repressive turn for women's rights and reproductive freedom. In the following viewpoint, the Center for Reproductive Rights (CRR) recaps the many extreme measures state legislatures proposed to restrict reproductive rights. Some states have passed requirements for intrusive, forced ultrasounds as well as mandatory counseling for women seeking an abortion. Doctors must read from scripts that are biased and inaccurate. Insurance laws like the Nelson Amendment gave states the authority to ban abortion coverage from state ACA exchanges. Lastly, ballot initiatives sought to mandate parental consent and imbue a fetus with "personhood" status.

Every year, anti-choice state legislators propose measures intended to restrict women's access to abortion, including mandatory delays, biased counseling provisions and other burdensome and unnecessary requirements.

"A First Look Back at 2010 State Legislative Session," Center for Reproductive Rights—Reproductiverights.org, August 27, 2010. Reprinted by Permission.

On average, more than six hundred bills are proposed annually and dozens are passed, making it increasingly difficult for women in many states to access abortion. 2010 has been one of the most challenging state legislative sessions for women's access to abortion in many years. States considered and enacted some of the most extreme restrictions on abortion in recent memory, as well as passing laws creating dozens of other significant new hurdles. At the same time, pro-choice legislators, advocates and governors continued to stand up for women's health and rights and in many cases defeated harmful legislation. As we begin to assess the impact of the 2010 session on women's access to reproductive health care, the Center offers this preliminary recap of some of the major trends and most onerous laws enacted this session.

Some of the Major Trends in 2010

Biased Counseling/Ultrasound
In 2010, as in the last several years, anti-choice proponents sought to enact dozens of "biased counseling" requirements, which compel physicians to provide patients with state-mandated information before a patient is permitted to obtain abortions. Under such laws, physicians and other health care professionals are obligated to give women who seek abortions information that may not be medically accurate or that may be inappropriate for her circumstances (such as telling a rape victim that the father may be liable for child support). Providers may also be required to read a script designed to dissuade women from having abortions.

Many of the more recently passed laws have included requirements that health care providers perform ultrasounds and offer patients the option to view the ultrasound image and hear a fetal heartbeat, or require patients to wait a specified period of time between receiving the state-mandated information and being permitted to obtain an abortion.

Ultrasound requirements are particularly demeaning to women, implying both that they do not understand their pregnancies and that they cannot make reasoned decisions without receiving information the state deems important. Women seeking abortions have carefully considered their options and life circumstances, and these requirements serve only as an attempt to shame them and make them feel guilty about their decisions.

For women who have wanted pregnancies or who have been victims of rape, incest, or abuse, these requirements can also result in unnecessary emotional suffering. These bills also interfere with the doctor/patient relationship, forcing physicians to give each woman "one size fits all" treatment, instead of allowing the physician to treat each patient individually according to his or her professional judgment.

Exchange Bans

This year, the debate over abortion in federal health care reform was a major impetus for aggressive efforts in the states. In March, Congress passed and the President signed the Patient Protection and Affordable Care Act (PPACA). Included in this Act was a section, commonly referred to as the "Nelson Amendment" after its sponsor, Sen. Ben Nelson (D.-Neb.), that restricts the means by which insurers can offer insurance coverage for abortion in the state insurance exchanges that will be created by 2014. In addition to imposing these restrictions, the Nelson Amendment also explicitly gave states the ability to ban abortion coverage from state exchanges altogether.

Two important and troubling aspects of the Congressional fight over abortion in the PPACA emerged. First, opponents' claim that abortion is not an essential and fundamental part of access to comprehensive health care further threatened to stigmatize and burden the right to an abortion. Yet access to abortion is essential to women's ability to protect their health and well-being throughout their reproductive years. It is also an extraordinarily common procedure: By the age of forty-five, approximately one in three women in this country will have had an abortion.[i]

Health organizations including the World Health Organization, the American College of Obstetricians and Gynecologists, the American Public Health Association, and the Association of Reproductive Health Professionals recognize abortion as a critical part of comprehensive reproductive health care.[ii] Anti-abortion activists and legislators ignored that fact, and instead used the health care reform process to further restrict women's access to abortion.

Second, the Nelson Amendment explicitly invited anti-choice state legislators to act by emphasizing in law that states could prohibit abortion coverage in the state-based exchanges created by the reform. As discussed below, several states have already taken up that invitation and passed bills banning insurance coverage in the not-yet-created state exchanges.

While passage of the PPACA occurred relatively late in the 2009-2010 state legislative season, reaction in the states was immediate. Although many legislatures were nearing the end of their sessions and had passed important bill-filing deadlines, ten states began immediately to consider bills banning or limiting insurance coverage for abortion in the not-yet-created state exchanges.[iii]

Moreover, while the Nelson Amendment (and other federal restrictions on abortion) contains exceptions for abortions sought by victims of rape and incest or in situations where the life of the woman is threatened, several states considered bans on coverage that would extend beyond federal law, sometimes banning coverage altogether. By the middle of July, when most legislatures had adjourned for the year, five states had enacted "exchange bans" (Arizona, Louisiana, Mississippi, Missouri, Tennessee) and bills containing such bans passed in the legislatures in Florida and Oklahoma before being vetoed by those states' governors.

The language of these bills varied. Some banned insurance coverage for abortion with no exceptions at all, while others incorporated a range of exceptions addressing health, life, rape and incest. One bill, in Louisiana, initially included a ban on abortion coverage in all insurance plans in the state, both inside and outside of the exchange. The bills introduced this session were no doubt just a preview of what the 2011 legislative session will bring.

Ballot Initiatives in 2010-2011:
Personhood and Parental Notice

Although most restrictions on women's access to abortion are enacted in state legislatures, there is a movement among anti-abortion activists to resort to state ballot initiatives, often to push an extreme agenda that would likely fail if proposed in the legislature. Unlike a statute that must be passed by both houses of a legislature and signed by a governor, a ballot measure can be placed on the ballot if a group can collect a sufficient number of signatures and, once on the ballot, can typically be passed by a majority of voters in the next election. Thus far this year, one ballot measure aimed at restricting reproductive rights has been passed and another will be on the ballot in November.

On August 24th, Alaska voters approved a measure that will require that before a young woman can have an abortion her physician must give notice to one of her parents at least 48 hours before the procedure. Even for a young woman in an abusive home, the only way to avoid this notification will be to seek a court order or to get a signed, notarized statement from a law enforcement officer or one of a small qualifying group of family members attesting to personal knowledge of the abuse. This new law's mandate of parental notification interferes with families and places the most vulnerable young women in even more danger, at risk of violence or of endangering their health through delay or by attempting to end the pregnancy themselves through dangerous means.

In addition to Alaska's parental involvement initiative, this year saw a new trend arise among ballot initiatives: so-called "personhood" measures. These proposals would amend state constitutions to recognize life from the moment of conception and to endow fertilized eggs, zygotes and fetuses with the status of a "person" under the law. Not only would such measures unconstitutionally ban abortion, they would also ban many forms of birth control and could result in the end of assisted reproductive technology, such as in-vitro fertilization (IVF). Furthermore, such measures would have unintended and unpredictable impacts on thousands of state laws that use the word "person."

At the start of 2010, "personhood" ballot initiative campaigns had begun to take shape in at least nine states. However, by August, only two proposals had received enough signatures to be placed on the ballot, in Colorado for the November 2010 election, and in Mississippi for November 2011.

Notably, in 2008, Colorado was the first state to consider a personhood initiative and voters overwhelmingly rejected it, 73 percent to 27 percent. In addition, the Mississippi ballot initiative is now the subject of a pre-election court challenge.

[...]

Conclusion

At this point in the year, 2010 has already seen many restrictive laws enacted. The Center for Reproductive Rights will continue to analyze the impact of this year's legislation on women's reproductive health and rights, and to work with advocates and legislators to oppose any similar legislation proposed in the future.

[...]

Notes

i. Guttmacher Institute, "An Overview of Abortion in the United States," http://www
.guttmacher.com/media/presskits/2005/06/28/abortionoverview.html (last visited July
28, 2010).

ii. American College of Gynecologists and Obstetricians, Guidelines for Women's
Health Care: A Resource Manual 431-32 (2007); Association of Reproductive Health
Professionals, Position Statements: Abortion, http://www.arhp.org/about-us/position
-statements#1 (last visited July 28, 2010); American Public Health Association (APHA),
Policy Statement, Need for State Legislation Protecting and Enhancing Women's Ability
to Obtain Safe, Legal Abortion Services Without Delay or Government Interference,
Oct. 28, 2008, available at http://www.apha.org/advocacy/policy/policysearch/default
.htm?id=1369; World Health Organization (WHO), WHO: Preventing Unsafe
Abortion, http://www.who.int/reproductivehealth/topics/unsafe_abortion/hrpwork/en
/index.html (last visited July 28, 2010).

iii. The states that considered or passed exchange bans in 2010 were: Arizona, Florida,
Georgia, Louisiana, Michigan, Mississippi, Missouri, Oklahoma, South Carolina,
Tennessee.

2

Reproductive Rights in the Age of President Trump

Emily Crockett

Emily Crockett is a freelance writer who has covered gender and other issues as a staff writer for Vox Media. She's also written about politics for outlets like Rewire and Campus Progress.

In the following viewpoint, Emily Crockett predicts what may be in store for both advocates and opponents of reproductive rights in light of Trump's victory. Trump has pledged to appoint Supreme Court justices who are hostile to reproductive rights. Advocates worry this could jeopardize Roe v. Wade. *Vice President Mike Pence is a longtime abortion opponent who has sought to defund Planned Parenthood for decades. Though abortion rights defenders fear for the future, they are not going down without a fight, and they have scored some encouraging wins with recent Supreme Court decisions.*

Advocates for reproductive health and rights are bracing for a big fight as soon as Donald Trump takes office.

Trump has promised to appoint "pro-life" justices to the Supreme Court who could overturn *Roe v. Wade*. His administration will be full of people like Tom Price—who would lead the nation's health department while opposing basic health coverage for women under the Affordable Care Act—and Vice President-elect Mike Pence,

"2017 Will Be a Big Year for Reproductive Rights. Here's What Will Happen, and What's at Stake," by Emily Crockett, Vox Media, January 6, 2017. Reprinted by Permission.

who was once the Congress member responsible for launching the GOP's war on Planned Parenthood in the first place.

Whatever 2017 has in store for reproductive rights, it will be eventful. But as big a challenge as the Trump administration poses to pro-choice advocates, the fight won't be as one-sided as you might think.

Congress Could Really, Actually Defund Planned Parenthood This Time. Will it?

Speaker of the House Paul Ryan said Thursday morning that before this year is out, Republicans in Congress will, in fact, seek to defund Planned Parenthood at the same time that they repeal the Affordable Care Act—using a budget reconciliation process that Democrats will be powerless to stop unless at least a few Republicans join them.

The move wouldn't kill off Planned Parenthood, but it *would* mean cutting off basic health care options for hundreds of thousands of women. Planned Parenthood's $500 million in federal funding doesn't come in a lump sum, and it doesn't cover abortion; it's paid out through Medicaid reimbursements and family planning grants, which cover services like birth control or cervical cancer screening. That means the mostly low-income women who rely on those programs would suffer the harshest consequences of defunding.

It's hardly a secret that the GOP has been trying for years to defund Planned Parenthood and repeal the ACA. It's also hard to say whether they can muster the unified political will to go through with it: Planned Parenthood is actually quite popular, whereas taking health insurance away from 20 million Americans probably won't be.

The exact details of both the "defunding" bill and the ACA "repeal" aren't clear yet. If Republicans keep both promises, though, it will be a double-whammy for women's health: gutting the nation's family planning safety net, plus denying women the ACA's comprehensive, no-cost coverage for preventive health care.

Congress Might Also Pass a National Abortion Ban That Challenges *Roe v. Wade*

With Republican House and Senate majorities, and a president who seems more than willing to go along with their socially conservative agenda, it wouldn't be at all surprising to see the reappearance of national proposals to ban abortion before a fetus is viable outside the womb—which would directly violate the Supreme Court's 1973 decision in *Roe v. Wade* and could trigger a high-stakes court challenge to that decision.

Two such laws were introduced in Congress last year and may appear again this year. One would ban the safest, most common method of second-trimester abortion; another would ban almost all abortion after 20 weeks of pregnancy.

The GOP's high-profile attempt to pass the 20-week ban last year fell apart when Republicans disagreed on how to handle rape exceptions. The bill also stood no chance of being signed by President Barack Obama or overcoming a Democratic filibuster in the Senate.

The Democratic filibuster could definitely still block bills like these in 2017 and beyond—assuming Republicans don't change the rules, that is. But there's also no telling which bills might get attached to must-pass legislation, or get forced through in other ways.

One big caveat, though: Even if one of these bills passed, it's still unlikely that the Court would uphold the law—much less use it as a tool to overturn *Roe v. Wade*. After all, the Court still has a five-justice majority that just voted to strengthen abortion rights in 2016. And the power of precedent is strong enough that even Chief Justice John Roberts might be reluctant to overturn a decision as well-established as *Roe*.

Still, that calculus could change dramatically if Trump gets the chance to appoint two or three new justices instead of one.

The Pro-choice Movement Is Going on Offense, and It Could Score Some Big Wins Even in the Trump Era

The stakes for abortion rights in America are already high. State restrictions have been slowly eroding the landscape of abortion access for decades—but a flood of new restrictions since 2010 (when Republicans swept state legislatures in the midterm elections) has made abortion access, in some states, not much better than in the days before *Roe v Wade.*

In the courts, though, reproductive rights advocates are already using this summer's big pro-choice Supreme Court victory to fight some of those new (and even old) laws. In states like Wisconsin, Mississippi, Louisiana, Alabama, Indiana, and Florida, the new Supreme Court case has helped block laws that would have forced clinics to close, or would have put other unconstitutional "undue burdens" on women seeking an abortion. There will be more of these kinds of legal fights, and possibly a lot more pro-choice wins, to come in 2017.

Also in 2017, many states are likely to continue a growing trend of passing bills to *expand* reproductive rights, rather than restrict them. The Center for Reproductive Rights tracked nearly 300 bills in 2016 that would expand or improve access to reproductive health care services.

Bills that make it easier for women to get birth control are a major trend right now; nearly every state considered, and eight states passed, some kind of pro-contraception bill. These include allowing pharmacists to dispense birth control without a prescription (which is already the law in California and Oregon, and passed this year in red-state Tennessee); allowing women to pick up a 6- or 12-month supply of birth control in one pharmacy visit (passed in Maryland, Vermont, Hawaii, and Illinois), to codifying and expanding ACA-style contraceptive benefits at the state level

(Maryland banned co-pays for contraception and sterilization). These kinds of laws could be especially important if Republicans get rid of Obamacare's coverage for women's health.

The intense attacks on reproductive rights in recent years have sprung advocates out of a decades-long defensive crouch. Now they are proactively fighting for abortion to be treated as a routine medical practice and a basic human right for women, not some shameful secret.

Planned Parenthood is launching a huge campaign to fight back against the defunding threats against it in Congress. Most Americans favor Planned Parenthood—and astonishingly, almost half of Trump supporters oppose defunding it. It's conceivable that enough public pressure could have a real impact.

Meanwhile, a national campaign is pushing harder than ever to restore federal funding for abortion by repealing the Hyde amendment. The Hyde amendment, activists say, discriminates against low-income women and women of color in particular and makes it harder for them to afford an abortion.

Repealing Hyde would have been an achievable goal under Hillary Clinton—but that doesn't mean activists are letting up the pressure under Trump. Far from it: The All Above All campaign to repeal the Hyde amendment just announced a six-figure ad buy in Washington, DC, urging lawmakers to "be bold" by ending the 40-year ban and saying that women won't be "punished"—a reference to Trump's infamous line about what might happen to women if *Roe v. Wade* were overturned.

Meanwhile, States Will Keep Passing More Anti-abortion Laws

States have passed 338 abortion restrictions in just the past six years, according to the Guttmacher Institute, a research organization for reproductive rights. That's 30 percent of the 1,142 laws that states have passed to limit abortion since *Roe v. Wade* was decided in 1973.

In 2016 alone, 18 states enacted 50 new abortion restrictions. It's a steady trend that certainly won't vanish overnight.

And if Congress can't or won't defund Planned Parenthood, a bunch of states will try to do it themselves. At least 24 have already tried in one way or another, and many have succeeded. But some of those efforts, like in Florida this year, have been blocked because they're illegal; kicking Planned Parenthood out of Medicaid, for instance, violates patients' right under federal law to receive family planning services from the health care provider of their choice.

Some States Have Already Passed So Many Anti-abortion Laws, They Need to Think of New Ones. But They Will.

The Guttmacher Institute identifies 10 major types of abortion restrictions that states most often pass:

- Medically inaccurate or misleading pre-abortion "counseling"
- Medically unnecessary waiting periods that sometimes require two trips to the clinic
- Medically unnecessary ultrasounds before an abortion
- Banning state Medicaid funds from covering abortion except in cases of life (but not health) endangerment, rape, or incest
- Restricting abortion coverage in private health plans
- Imposing medically inappropriate restrictions on medication abortion
- Unnecessary regulations on abortion facilities that are difficult to comply with
- Imposing an unconstitutional ban on abortion before viability (like a 20-week ban) or limits on abortion after viability
- Preemptively banning abortion just in case *Roe v. Wade* is overturned

Guttmacher considers states that have passed four of these 10 laws "hostile" to reproductive rights, and "very hostile" if they've passed six or more. And in just the past decade, the number of "hostile" or "very hostile" states has skyrocketed.

If a state is already "very hostile" to reproductive rights, though, chances are that its lawmakers have already passed *most* of the restrictions they want. So the breakneck pace of lawmaking should slow down eventually.

Then again, sometimes it may not. Pro-life activists and lobbyists are constantly dreaming up new laws to limit abortion. And pro-life state legislators are usually game to try to pass them.

The Anti-abortion Movement Is Changing Tactics. Some of the Results Have Been Bizarre. 2017 Could Get Even Weirder.

Elizabeth Nash, state issues manager at the Guttmacher Institute, said she noticed "a big shift in rhetoric" in the pro-life movement in 2016. Instead of justifying abortion restrictions because they allegedly improve "women's health and safety," she said, activists have started using "more inflammatory language or graphic imagery" as their main argument against abortion rights.

In part, this trend was inspired by the propaganda videos that spun Planned Parenthood's fetal tissue donation program into an illegal, for-profit conspiracy to "sell baby parts." Not a single state, federal, or media investigation could substantiate the videos' claims—but they still had a huge influence on policy in 2016, and probably will in 2017 too.

Eight states banned fetal tissue donation or research in 2016. Indiana, Texas, and Louisiana tried (but ultimately failed in court) to require all fetal tissue to be cremated or buried—which was both an indirect way of banning fetal tissue donation, and a visceral appeal to treat fetuses just like born-alive infants. (Ohio Attorney General Mike DeWine tried to promote a similar law using false, inflammatory claims that Planned Parenthood improperly threw "steam-cooked" aborted fetuses into landfills.)

Gross-out posters and protest tactics aren't new. But gross-out *policy* seems to be getting more common. Instead of quietly regulating abortion out of existence using obscure "admitting privileges" or "ambulatory surgical center" laws, anti-abortion activists are shifting back to visceral, often misleading rhetoric that both humanizes the fetus and demonizes abortion.

In 2016 Indiana and Louisiana tried, and failed in court, to ban abortions that supposedly "discriminated" against a fetus based on race, sex, or genetic anomalies. Ohio joined 15 other states to ban abortion after 20 weeks, based on a very medically dubious theory of "fetal pain." Four states banned the dilation and evacuation (D&E) procedure—the safest and most common method for performing a second-trimester abortion—and colorfully rebranded it as a "dismemberment abortion."

The D&E ban, which was blocked in Alabama and Louisiana but still stands in Mississippi and West Virginia, is basically an indirect ban on second-trimester abortion (after 14 weeks). It forces doctors to choose between not performing the procedure at all, losing their medical license for performing it correctly, or putting their patients at risk by using a legal, but less safe or reliable, method. Utah passed a similar indirect ban on abortions after 20 weeks, by passing a "fetal anesthesia" law that was pure medical gibberish.

Many of these laws are an obvious violation of *Roe v. Wade* because they ban or severely restrict abortion before a fetus is viable. But some of them are also just *bizarre*. Fetus funerals? Fantasy medical procedures? Suggesting that black women who get an abortion are actually engaging in racial discrimination?

In some ways, though, it's a strategic shift that makes sense. As long as *Roe v. Wade* stands, you can't legally block a woman from getting an abortion before her fetus is viable. You can regulate abortion to a certain extent—but as the Supreme Court affirmed this summer by striking down two major Texas laws, you can't pass bogus "regulations" that just close a bunch of clinics without improving health or safety.

So if what you *really* want is to outlaw abortion, pretty much all that's left after that decision is finding a different way to move the legal goalposts back. Find reasons that the rights of the fetus might trump the rights of the woman *before* it can survive outside her body—by, say, convincing courts to replace the standard of "fetal viability" (which happens around 24 to 26 weeks of pregnancy, give or take, but has to be determined by a doctor) with "fetal pain" (a theory that defies credibility by claiming fetuses can feel pain at precisely 20 weeks of pregnancy).

The pro-life movement has been painted into a tricky legal corner, and its new fetus-focused strategy faces very long constitutional odds. Even though some new laws won't be challenged or struck down, they still won't do nearly as much to limit abortion access as the old "women's health and safety" laws did.

Then again, passing the weird new laws also means investing in a long shot that *just might* pay off someday, and even reverse *Roe v. Wade.*

3

Abortion Is Legal and Saying Otherwise Is Counterproductive

Bridgette Dunlap

Bridgette Dunlap is a lawyer and scholar, and a writer for several publications including Ms. *and* Rolling Stone. *Her work centers on public understanding of and access to legal systems.*

In the following viewpoint, attorney Bridgette Dunlap cautions liberals against rhetoric that suggests Roe v. Wade *is not the law of the land. Doubts about the legality of abortion can become a self-fulfilling prophecy. Using the analogous case of* Heller v. District of Columbia, *Dunlap argues that public opinion concerning the right to bear arms influenced how the high court interpreted the Second Amendment. If pro-choice advocates downplay abortion's constitutionality, it becomes easier for this to change. Anti-choice advocates cannot use the law to prevent abortion, however they can (and do) make abortions more costly and inaccessible. Those who ignore this distinction do so at their peril.*

Political elites on the left have a history of telling the public that whether the Constitution protects abortion is an open question. Raising the specter of *Roe v. Wade* being overturned or gutted is a time-honored tactic for rallying the base. But with the Supreme Court hearing *Whole Woman's Health v. Hellerstedt* today and Justice Antonin Scalia's death turning constitutional

"Abortion Is a Constitutional Right. We Need to Stop Talking Like It Isn't," by Bridgette Dunlap, *Ms.* Magazine, March 2, 2016. Reprinted by Permission.

interpretation into a campaign issue, it is time to abandon the defeatist rhetoric. Claiming that the right to abortion is on shakier legal ground than it actually is undermines established protections, because the way the Supreme Court interprets the Constitution tends to be consistent with how the public does.

Recent changes in Supreme Court doctrine brought to us by conservatives illustrate how much the public's view of the Constitution matters. In the 1970s, gun rights proponents decided the right to bear arms wasn't just for well-regulated state militias. Movement lawyers developed a new reading of the Second Amendment that NRA activists, movie stars and Republican politicians repeated for decades. Eventually the public came to believe the Constitution guaranteed an individual right to bear arms, despite the Supreme Court having long held it did not. Then, in the 2008 case *Heller v. District of Columbia*, the court adopted an interpretation in line with the public's and struck down D.C.'s handgun ban. Justice Scalia's opinion flipped the understanding of the Second Amendment: Individuals have the right to bear arms but (sorry, militias) not the ones you'd need to fight a tyrannical federal government.

The challenge to the Affordable Care Act showed how quickly this process can occur. When libertarian academics first floated the argument that requiring individuals to purchase health insurance violated the Commerce Clause, most legal scholars thought it was laughable. They refined the argument on blogs and op-ed pages, while Republican politicians took it viral. It became so accepted that not only did news organizations initially report that the ACA had been struck down, but five justices adopted the Commerce Clause argument that had been considered frivolous only three years prior. After widespread argument over the right to be free from government-mandated broccoli, both Chief Justice John Roberts and Justice Ruth Bader Ginsburg felt obliged to address it in their opinions upholding the mandate.

But unlike conservatives making constitutional demands without precedent to back them up, liberals do the opposite—

telling the public they're unsure whether the Constitution protects abortion, no matter how many times the court says it does.

In 1992, the country was amid a presidential election and *Planned Parenthood v. Casey* was at the Supreme Court. Reproductive rights advocates, hoping to build support for Democratic candidates and the Freedom of Choice Act, told the public the court was about to overturn *Roe*.

Instead, Justices Sandra Day O'Connor, Anthony Kennedy and David Souter authored a plurality opinion holding that a woman's right to terminate her pregnancy before viability "is a rule of law and a component of liberty we cannot renounce." The Fourteenth Amendment liberty rights that protect it—the right to bodily integrity and the right to make fundamental decisions about family—were recognized by the court long before *Roe*.

Casey did, however, uphold regulations requiring counseling, a waiting period and parental involvement for minors seeking abortions. Perhaps due to pro-choice leaders framing abortion as a family-privacy right—on the advice of pollsters—and downplaying a woman's right to personal autonomy (as Will Saletan documented in *Bearing Right*), even people who identified as pro-choice saw these paternalistic restrictions as reasonable and constitutional.

But when *Casey* came down, pro-choice leaders told the public *Roe* might as well have been overturned. Prominent liberals have repeated the story that *Casey* is worthless and *Roe*'s days are numbered in the decades since. Fear is a good way to get people engaged, but it's dangerous to say your rights aren't secure under current doctrine because people might believe you.

Today, we are again in the middle of a presidential election with an extremely important abortion case at the Supreme Court and liberals warning of doom: If a Republican president is elected, we probably just celebrated the last anniversary of *Roe*. The court's decision in *Whole Woman's Health* may end legal abortion in red states. *Roe* could be dead by June.

Whole Woman's Health challenges two provisions of Texas' omnibus abortion bill known as HB2. The bill would close any clinic that isn't an ambulatory surgical center and prohibit doctors without hospital admitting privileges from performing abortions for no medical reason. Ten clinics, at most, would remain if the provisions are upheld, making ending a pregnancy a Sisyphean ordeal for women who live hundreds of miles from a clinic.

Commentators on the left tend to acknowledge that these are bogus health regulations meant to shut down clinics, but treat whether they are constitutional under the court's precedent as a close question. It is not.

Casey allowed states greater leeway to regulate abortion so long as those regulations do not place an "undue burden" on the woman's right to end her pregnancy before viability. Laws encouraging women to give birth must be "calculated to inform the woman's free choice, not hinder it" because the ultimate decision remains hers. Though *Casey* was primarily about laws purported to promote the state's interest in potential life rather than women's health, the justices anticipated the strategy of using "unnecessary health regulations" to make ending a pregnancy arduous and expensive and said that would be a no-go.

The undue burden standard isn't a paragon of clarity, but it isn't as useless as critics say it is—and abortion opponents want it to be. *Whole Woman's Health* is an easy case. Legal scholars—including leading conservatives who have argued *Roe* was wrongly decided—have explained that the appellate court's decision upholding the challenged provisions of HB2 cannot be squared with *Casey*.

But rather than saying HB2 is blatantly unconstitutional and the court needs to strike it down, liberal politicians and commentators keep telling us to be afraid. Hillary Clinton says she's worried. But instead of fretting, the nation's most famous woman lawyer might consider reminding the public that the Constitution protects a woman's right end to her pregnancy without undue interference from the government and explaining that the court's precedent does not allow the catastrophe HB2 would be for Texas women.

Some commentators imply that whether HB2 violates *Casey* is barely relevant to the outcome of the case because swing vote Justice

Kennedy thinks abortion is immoral, or holds patriarchal views toward women, or is just an unprincipled guy. Jeffrey Toobin tells us there is "every reason to believe" Kennedy will vote to uphold HB2 as though no law applies or Kennedy is likely to ignore it. Those who hold a low opinion of Justice Kennedy could at least do us the favor of holding him accountable by acknowledging that he would have to upend his own opinion in *Casey* to uphold HB2.

That is not likely. The portions of the *Casey* opinion that explain how constitutional protections for abortion are much broader than the right to privacy are commonly attributed to Justice Kennedy. *Casey* is the foundation of Kennedy's liberty jurisprudence protecting gay rights.

Even the conservative justices might vote to strike down HB2. This isn't an abortion case in the typical sense—the state of Texas denies the challenged provisions are meant to protect fetal life. The idea that the state can regulate you out of business as long as it makes some implausible claim about health and safety should alarm conservatives. Anyone who cares about the Constitution and the rule of law should be appalled by a state using obviously pretextual laws to so severely curtail a constitutional right. At the time of this writing, FantasySCOTUS predicts that nearly every justice will vote to strike down HB2.

So what's so bad about scaring the base a little if the case is a winner and everyone will be pleasantly surprised?

The immediate problem is that if the public believes that the court upholding HB2 is a likely possibility, rather than the radical departure from precedent it would be, the justices have more room to maneuver. It will look like a nice compromise to strike down HB2 because it is unusually flagrant and harmful, but fail to define the undue burden standard in a way that provides meaningful protection against an array of current and future attacks on abortion access.

As Judge Richard Posner explained in an opinion striking down Wisconsin's admitting privileges requirement, a burden is undue if it is "disproportionate or gratuitous." Even a slight burden imposed by a health regulation that does not address a legitimate safety issue should be considered undue. Yet, liberals help abortion opponents move the goalposts in the opposite direction by repeating the unsupported claim that *Casey* allowed states such vast freedom to burden women that HB2 just might fly.

The larger problem is that after decades of similar hyperbole, we have a discourse on abortion that proceeds as though there are no constitutional boundaries.

Treating *Roe* being overturned as a credible threat has obscured the actual attacks on abortion in this country—which are on its availability and affordability, not its legality. Worse, this story perpetuates the conservative narrative that there is something illegitimate about the right. If *Roe* can be overturned any minute or has already been gutted, then it isn't a real constitutional right and no abortion restriction is off the table. *Roe* alarmism is an effective way to amass votes, donations or pageviews, but it contradicts the reality that abortion opponents are "foreclosed from using the machinery of government to ban abortions in early term," as Justice Kennedy has put it. The court has said abortion opponents may use persuasion but not the force of law to stop a woman from having an abortion, but liberals keep encouraging the public not to take that seriously.

More than 40 years after *Roe*, Republican presidential candidates debate various unconstitutional abortion policies while Democrats indulge them. Engaging the merits of proposals that are off the table as a matter of longstanding precedent by calling out callousness towards rape victims or explaining the tragic medical reasons women need abortions after 20 weeks only legitimizes the false notion that there is no settled law when it comes to abortion. Every 20-week ban challenged in court has been struck down and the Supreme Court recently declined two invitations to reconsider the viability line without a single justice publicly dissenting. If liberals can't even articulate the bright line rule that pre-viability bans are unconstitutional, they aren't going to get the public to understand that less absolute barriers are the real threat, and equally unconstitutional.

No one is proposing we ban handguns because it is understood that would violate a right only recently recognized by the Supreme Court. For abortion to become an accessible medical service instead of a wedge issue, liberals need to stop calling the existence of the right into doubt. They should start talking about abortion like the well-established right "central to personal autonomy and dignity" that the court has held it is—and demanding legal protections befitting of it.

4

Many States Are Hostile Toward Abortion Rights

Carrie Levi

Chicago-based writer Carrie Levi has written extensively about abortion rights for Spiked, *a British online news magazine.*

In the following viewpoint, Carrie Levi chronicles the statewide reproductive rights landscape in the United States today. Even though a woman's right to an abortion is constitutionally protected, states have recently passed a spate of laws regulating and restricting abortion access. For example, Texas passed building requirements that the AMA says have nothing to do with abortion safety. Mississippi has only one remaining abortion clinic, and Oklahoma encourages misinformation and obsolete medical techniques. Finally, in Kansas, anti-choice militants turned to violence, murdering the well-known doctor George Tiller while he was attending a church service. These and other methods are used by hostile states to limit abortion access.

When it comes to shutting down women's rights, these 10 states are way ahead of the curve. It wasn't easy picking 10—there are simply too many worthy contenders. All I can say is, well done guys. From bombings to the murder of an abortion doctor in his church to a representative comparing women to livestock—not to mention an epidemic of well-funded politicians attempting to

"The 10 Worst US States for Abortion Rights," by Carrie Levi, *Spiked*, February 17, 2015. Reprinted by Permission.

legislate abortion out of existence, one state at a time—the anti-abortion landscape in the US has reached new heights.

Abortion has been legal in the US since *Roe vs Wade*, the landmark 1973 Supreme Court ruling that established, with various caveats, the right to abortion. But you wouldn't know it these days. In the past four years, 231 new restrictions on abortion have been enacted at the state level—more than in the previous decade. Politicians across the country are utilising cunning legal manoeuvres to regulate abortion, severely limiting women's access to safe and legal care. Unable completely to ban the "business of abortion," they seem to be trying to take it down—one state at a time.

10) Kansas

Formerly home to one of the country's few late-term abortion providers, Kansas has quite a volatile history with regard to women's rights. Dr George Tiller and his clinic became something of a battleground for anti-abortion activism. Tiller was infamously branded "Tiller the Baby Killer," a nickname that political pundits, including Bill O'Reilly, regularly used for him. For three decades the anti-abortion movement tried to shut down his practice with lawsuits, regulatory complaints and a summer-long protest in 1991, which resulted in 2,000 arrests. Tiller's clinic was bombed, his wife was assaulted in the clinic parking lot, and, in 1993, he was wounded in both arms when five shots were fired as he left his clinic. In 2009, while handing out programmes in his church at Sunday service, he was shot in the head and killed. Tiller's clinic remains closed to this day, leaving only three clinics in the entire state. Subsequently, Kansas lawmakers have pursued legislation to keep the University of Kansas Medical Center from providing abortion training for its medical residents.

9) North and South Dakota

In 2011, South Dakota state representative Phil Jensen sponsored a bill that could have made killing in order to defend the life of a fetus "justifiable homicide." The pro-choice community feared such a law could be interpreted as the legalisation of killing abortion doctors. Defending the bill in an interview with Greg Sargent of the *Washington Post*, Jensen argued that the bill only concerned illegal acts. When asked what the purpose of the law was, if not to target abortion providers, Jensen provided the following example: "Say an ex-boyfriend, who happens to be father of a baby, doesn't want to pay child support for the next 18 years and he beats on his ex-girlfriend's abdomen in trying to abort her baby. If she did kill him, it would be justified. She is resisting an effort to murder her unborn child." Jensen seemed unconcerned and dismissive of the suggestion that the law could have the potential to incite anti-abortion extremists.

In North Dakota in 2013, governor Jack Dalrymple attempted to enforce a ban on abortion after six weeks of pregnancy, a time when many women do not yet know they are pregnant. After a federal judge blocked the law, calling it "invalid and unconstitutional," the governor said it was "a legitimate attempt by a state legislature to discover the boundaries of *Roe vs Wade*."

8) Mississippi

Only one abortion clinic remains open in the entire state of Mississippi—and governor Phil Bryant is currently doing everything he can to shut it down. "On this unfortunate anniversary of *Roe vs Wade*, my goal is to end abortion in Mississippi," he said in a speech last month. He also made headlines recently when he tried to impose a law requiring abortion doctors to have admitting privileges at local hospitals. Bryant's proposal is one of the popular new "TRAP Laws" (targeted regulation of abortion providers) now being tabled by anti-choice politicians. As the Center for Reproductive Rights has argued, such regulations are unnecessary, as abortion is in fact one of medicine's safest procedures. Instead the regulation seems aimed at making it increasingly difficult for abortion providers to function. While attempting to comply with the new regulations, the doctors at Jackson Women's Health Organisation have been unable to obtain such privileges at seven local hospitals. After making national headlines, this law has been temporarily blocked, pending the court's final decision—allowing the clinic, for now, to remain open.

7) Georgia

Farmer and Georgia state representative Terry England famously supported a bill in 2012 which tried to ban abortions after 20 weeks—with no exceptions for the life of the mother, or a non-viable fetus. England made headlines when he took to the microphone in support of the bill and relayed his experience on the farm of delivering dead calves and pigs. "It breaks our hearts to see those animals not make it," he said. But, he went on, "life hands us many experiences." His comments led his opponents to rename the legislation the "Women as Livestock" bill. The bill was passed by the House of Representatives and approved by the Senate—causing several female representatives to walk out—but it was later blocked by a judge and is not currently in effect.

6) Texas

Squelching women's reproductive rights is something of a speciality of the southern state of Texas—home to some of the most stringent abortion restrictions in the country. In 2013, then governor Rick Perry proposed a package of abortion restrictions which severely limited women's access to abortion throughout the state—causing a significant number of clinics to close when they didn't meet, among other things, new building specifications for existing clinics. The Center for Reproductive Rights says the required renovations (expanding hallway widths and ceiling heights, adding locker rooms and parking spaces) do nothing to improve safety and are opposed by the American Medical Association.

In opposition to Perry's restrictions, state senator Wendy Davis staged an 11-hour filibuster, speaking late into the night to prevent the vote from happening. Perry, however, called a second special session the following day, successfully passing the bills and signing them into law. This caused all but eight abortion clinics in the state to close. Some clinics have been allowed to reopen temporarily, pending a final decision by the courts.

If that wasn't enough, Texas also requires that abortion clinics carry out medically unnecessary transvaginal sonograms and counselling which includes information on the purported link between abortion and breast cancer, mental-health consequences and fetal pain—all of which are refuted by much of the scientific community.

5) Florida

State-issued "Choose Life" license plates are available to Florida residents. Florida politicians have passed a bill that redistributes funds from these plates and their annual renewal fees to anti-abortion organisations. Florida has attempted to block all state funding to Planned Parenthood organisations. Meanwhile, Choose Life America, which started in Florida in 2000, has raised more than $21 million nationally.

4) Louisiana

While state-level bans on abortion are still illegal in the US, states eager for that day to end have implemented "bans-in-waiting." Louisiana is one such state, and has a law in place that would immediately outlaw abortion in the event that *Roe vs Wade* is overturned. Americans United for Life, which offers legislators model anti-choice guidelines, has ranked Louisiana number-one on its list of pro-life states five years in a row.

3) Oklahoma

With only three abortion clinics in total, the panhandle state is particularly hostile to women's reproductive rights. Last year, Oklahoma governor Mary Fallin signed a bill into law attempting to place restrictions on medical abortion, requiring providers to follow obsolete methods. Under the new rules, patients are required to take three times more medication than the American College of Obstetricians and Gynecologists recommends, warranting additional visits to the clinic. The law also sought completely to ban medical abortion after seven weeks of pregnancy, instead of the usual nine to 10 week limit, requiring women to undergo surgical abortions instead.

2) Illinois

Usually falling somewhere in the middle on the issue of abortion, Illinois isn't an obvious choice for this list. However, it is home to controversial anti-choice activist Eric Scheidler, executive director of the Pro-Life Action League. Last month, on the forty-second anniversary of *Roe vs Wade*, Scheidler mailed a package to every abortion clinic in the country containing a pair of plastic handcuffs, a photo of an abortion doctor being arrested, and a note that said "Could you be next?" Defending his stunt, Scheidler said: "I am working towards a day when abortion is a crime and committing the crime of abortion would result in an abortionist being arrested." Asked whether he also sent handcuffs to women who terminated pregnancies, Scheidler said: "Certainly not. For one thing, I don't have that mailing list."

1) Arizona

Where some states have tried to pass anti-abortion measures and failed, Arizona seems particularly committed to seeing that they prevail. Over 40 Arizona statutes address abortion in some way. When a constituent sent an email urging state representative Terri Proud to vote against two such bills in 2012, she responded: "Until the dead child can tell me that she/he does not feel any pain, I have no intentions of clearing the conscience of the living. I will be voting YES."

ACA Repeal Would Strip Women of Contraceptive Coverage

Amie Newman

Amie Newman is a Seattle-based writer and communications expert dedicated to helping social change organizations. She is a board member of NARAL Pro-Choice WA and has also worked with the Bill & Melinda Gates Foundation.

In the following viewpoint, Amie Newman argues that the Affordable Care Act's provision for preventative women's health services and full financial coverage of at least one method of contraception have been successful. The provision has saved money for individual women and has also saved the government billions of dollars. More important, it has reduced the amount of unwanted pregnancies and abortions. Without affordable access to birth control, women's lives and health suffer. Thus, efforts in the House, Senate, and White House to repeal the ACA directly threaten the many hard won gains for women's health and reproductive rights.

Kylie Sparks is a young actress who suffers from a range of medical issues from fibromyalgia to irregular and painful menstrual cycles. Her period was so agonizing that she says, "There were 3 to 5 days a month where I would have to cancel auditions or meetings because not even my strongest prescription pain medication could touch these." She couldn't use oral birth control (a common treatment for irregular cycles) because she developed blood clots. Before the implementation of the Affordable Care Act (ACA), and its mandate that private and public health insurance plans cover FDA-approved birth control at no cost, she says she had to put off medical appointments she needed for other conditions just to get treatment for her painful periods. "This was all before the ACA, so these costs, even with health insurance, were ridiculous," she wrote me in an email.

Kylie told me that her life drastically changed after the ACA passed. Her doctor listened to her medical history and recommended the Mirena IUD, which can act as both a birth control method and remedy for her painful and irregular periods (and lasts 5 years). With the ACA it was free for her. It changed her life, Kylie said.

Now that Congress has taken its first steps to repeal the Affordable Care Act—also known as Obamacare—millions of women across the U.S. are wondering how they are going to pay for their contraception if the provision for birth control disappears, with no adequate replacement.

The ACA requires that a range of preventative women's health services—including mammograms, screenings for sexually transmitted infections, and HPV vaccinations—are covered in full, with no co-pay. Contraception is a preventative service and so 18 categories of FDA-approved birth control methods are required to be covered by health insurance plans, including Medicaid, as long as they are prescribed by a health care provider.

The provision isn't perfect. It requires that insurance plans make at least one type of birth control available to women, from each of the 18 categories, at no-cost. So, for example, if a particular brand of birth control pill doesn't work for an individual and her plan only covers that one at no-cost, she may need to cover the cost of a different type that works better for her. There are also exemptions to the law, most notably for religious employer health plans, that have resulted in multiple court battles. But overall the law has worked extraordinarily well, helped to eliminate gender disparities in health care costs, and made it easier for millions of women to access the full range of contraceptive methods.

How well, you ask? At of the end of 2015, more than 55 million women in the U.S. had contraceptive coverage. Since Obamacare was implemented in 2012, women have saved approximately $1.4 billion *per year* on birth control. The percentage of women with private insurance who pay nothing out of pocket for their birth control skyrocketed from 15% in 2012 to 67% in 2014. It also saves the government billions of dollars, in case you're wondering.

The rate of unintended pregnancies has also sharply declined over the last four years, as has the rate of abortions. These changes are likely due to women having access to affordable contraception, according to a Guttmacher Institute analysis. And, to be clear, although anti-abortion advocates want to point to increasing abortion restrictions on the state level for the reason abortions have declined—and it is true that restrictions to abortion access contribute to declines—the evidence suggests that improved access to contraception has made the biggest impact on these numbers. The abortion rate has declined in states with more abortion restrictions as well as those without. In fact, according to Guttmacher, over 60 percent of the decline in abortion numbers are in states *without* new abortion restrictions.

It's not news that contraception is good for women and their families. When women can decide if and when to have children and have the ability to space their pregnancies, their lives change for the better. In 2016, the Guttmacher Institute asked women about the birth control provision, and a majority reported that birth control has helped them take better care of themselves and their families, extend their education, and support themselves financially.

The birth control provision is also popular with the public. According to the Kaiser Family Foundation, the majority of Americans (71%) support laws that require health plans to cover the full cost of birth control. Even before the ACA was implemented, when the comment period was open for the public to weigh in on

Obamacare, the birth control provision received far and away the highest number of comments, with more than 300,000 women's health advocates in all 50 states supporting the effort.

With all of these positive consequences, there's a lot on the line if the federal requirement to cover no-cost birth control disappears. It could result in millions of women who can no longer afford to pay for contraception or pay for the most effective long-term methods. One year after Obamacare went into effect, Think Progress noted:

> Before Obamacare's birth control provision went into effect, the high cost of contraception was prohibitive for many women. In fact, research conducted in 2012 found that nearly half of young women said they hadn't used their birth control as directed in order to cut down on costs. And extremely small numbers of women opted to use the most effective form of contraception—the intrauterine device, or IUD—because it could cost several hundred dollars out of pocket.

If the contraceptive coverage mandate goes away, we'll once again put women in the U.S. at risk of not being able to afford the tools they need to help prevent unintended pregnancies, space wanted pregnancies, or manage health conditions like endometriosis.

The process of repealing the ACA is in motion and, as of now, President-Elect Trump and the GOP members of Congress who are at the forefront of the repeal push have not put forth a replacement idea. If it's repealed, the ACA won't go away until the end of 2017. But that doesn't leave women feeling much better. Although four states have expanded their coverage of contraception to include no-cost contraception for women with private insurance or Medicaid, if the federal birth control coverage requirement is thrown out, the majority of the 99% of women who rely on birth control at some point in their lives, and the families who depend upon affordable access to contraception for a multitude of reasons, will be left without a critical preventative health service, threatening women's health and the tremendous public health gains we've made in a relatively short period of time.

6

An ACA Repeal Impacts Specific Areas of Women's Health

Danielle Kurtzleben

Danielle Kurtzleben is a political reporter assigned to NPR's Washington desk. In her current role, she writes for NPR.org's It's All Politics blog, focusing on data visualizations.

In the following viewpoint, NPR correspondent Danielle Kurtzleben reviews what the Affordable Care Act (ACA) accomplished to positively impact women's health. Under the ACA, insurers are obligated to cover maternity care, contraceptives, and a variety of preventive services for women, and are no longer allowed to charge extra for such coverage. Despite the Republican promise to repeal and replace the ACA, these efforts have been unsuccessful. If some version of repeal were to eventually pass, it would leave maternity care and contraceptive coverage intact, but it would defund Planned Parenthood, making abortion unaffordable for many low-income women.

The Affordable Care Act changed women's health care in some big ways: It stopped insurance companies from charging women extra, forced insurers to cover maternity care and contraceptives and allowed many women to get those contraceptives (as well as a variety of preventive services, like Pap smears and mammograms) at zero cost.

Now Republicans have the opportunity to repeal that law, also known as Obamacare. But that doesn't mean all those things will go away. In fact, many will remain.

Confused? Here's a rundown of how this bill would change some women-specific areas of health care, what it wouldn't change, and what we don't know so far.

What Would Change:

Abortion coverage

There are restrictions on abortion under current law—the Hyde Amendment prohibits federal subsidies from being spent on abortions, except in the case of pregnancies that are the result of rape or incest or that threaten the life of the mother. So while health care plans can cover abortions, those being paid for with subsidies "must follow particular administrative requirements to ensure that no federal funds go toward abortion," as the Guttmacher Institute, which supports abortion rights, explains.

But the GOP bill tightens this. It says that the tax credits at the center of the plan cannot be spent at all on any health care plan that covers abortion (aside from the Hyde Amendment's exceptions). So while health care plans *can* cover abortion, very few people may be able to purchase those sorts of plans, as they wouldn't be able to use their tax credits on them. That could make it much more expensive and difficult to obtain an abortion under this law than under current law.

Planned Parenthood funding

This bill partially "defunds" Planned Parenthood, meaning it would cut back on the federal funding that can be used for services at the clinics. Fully 43 percent of Planned Parenthood's revenue in fiscal year 2015—more than $550 million—came from government grants and reimbursements.

Right now, under Obamacare, federal funds can be spent at Planned Parenthood, but they can't be used for abortion—again, a result of the Hyde Amendment and again, with the three Hyde Amendment exceptions. But this bill goes further, saying that people couldn't use Medicaid at Planned Parenthood.

To be clear, it's not that there's a funding stream going directly from the government to Planned Parenthood that Congress can just turn off. Rather, the program reimburses Planned Parenthood for the care it provides to Medicaid recipients. So this bill would mean that Medicaid recipients who currently receive care at an organization that provides abortions would have to find a new provider (whom Medicaid would then reimburse).

Abortion is a small part of what Planned Parenthood does: The organizations says it accounted for 3.4 percent of all services provided in the year ending in September 2014. (Of course, some patients receive more than one service; Planned Parenthood had around 2.5 million patients in that year. Assuming one abortion per patient, that's roughly 13 percent of all patients receiving abortions.)

Together, providing contraception and the testing for and treatment of sexually transmitted diseases made up three-quarters of the services the organization provided in one year.

That means low-income women (that is, women on Medicaid) could be among the most heavily affected by this bill, as it may force them to find other providers for reproductive health services.

Of the other government money that goes to Planned Parenthood, most of it comes from Title X. That federal program, created under President Richard Nixon, provides family planning services to people beyond Medicaid, like low-income women who are not Medicaid-eligible. Earlier this year, Republicans started the process of stripping that funding.

What Wouldn't Change (Yet):

Republicans have stressed that this bill was just one of three parts, so it's hard to say definitively what wouldn't change at all as a result of their plan. But thus far, here's what is holding steady:

Maternity and contraceptive coverage

Because this was a reconciliation bill, it could cover fiscal-related topics only. It couldn't get into many of the particulars of what people's coverage will look like, meaning some things won't change.

The essential health benefits set out in Obamacare—a list of 10 types of services that all plans must cover—do not change for other policies. Maternity care is included in those benefits, as is contraception, so plans will have to continue to cover those. The GOP bill also doesn't change the Obamacare policy that gave women access to free contraception, as Vox's Emily Crockett reported.

In addition, maternity and contraception are still both "mandatory benefits" under Medicaid. That doesn't change in the GOP bill. (Confusingly, the bill *does* sunset essential health benefits for Medicaid recipients. But because there is overlap and these particular benefits remain "mandatory," they aren't going away.)

However, all of this won't necessarily remain unchanged. In response to a question about defunding Planned Parenthood this week, Health and Human Services Secretary Tom Price said that he didn't want to "violate anybody's conscience." When a reporter asked how this relates to birth control, Price did not give a definite answer.

"We're working through all of those issues," he said. "As you know, many of those were through the rule-making process, and we're working through that. So that's not a part of this piece of legislation right here."

So this is something that could easily change in the second "phase" of the health care plan, when rules are changed.

"Preventative services [the category that includes contraception] hasn't been touched, but we expect those to be touched probably via regulation," said Laurie Sobel, associate director for women's health policy at the Kaiser Family Foundation.

The end of gender rating

Prior to Obamacare, women were often charged more for the same health plans as men. The rationale was that women tend to use more health care services than men.

However, Obamacare banned the practice, and that ban seems unlikely to change, as the GOP cites nondiscrimination as one of the bill's selling points:

"Our proposal specifically prohibits any gender discrimination. Women will have equal access to the same affordable, quality health care options as men do under our proposal."

7

Defunding Planned Parenthood Is a Priority for GOP Leaders

Julie Rovner

Julie Rovner is chief Washington correspondent at KHN. For sixteen years, she served as a health policy correspondent for NPR, where she helped lead the network's coverage of the passage and implementation of the Affordable Care Act.

Planned Parenthood provides essential health care services for women, many of whom live near or below the poverty line. These services include, but are not limited to, contraception and abortion. In the following viewpoint, Julie Rovner assesses longstanding threats to the organization's funding. As the nation's largest abortion provider, Planned Parenthood has been in the crosshairs of conservatives since the 1980s. Half of its budget comes from federal, state, and local governments, but defunding the organization will not be as easy as abortion foes would like. Stripping funding would require major changes to existing Medicaid laws. Although such changes may not pass the Senate, the fate of Planned Parenthood remains an open question.

If repealing the Affordable Care Act is the Republican Congress' job one, defunding Planned Parenthood is a close second.

In fact, the two priorities might be paired. House Speaker Paul Ryan, R-Wis., told reporters Jan. 5 that efforts to defund the

"That Vow to Defund Planned Parenthood: Easy to Say, Hard to Do," by Julie Rovner, Kaiser Health News, January 15, 2017. Reprinted by Permission.

organization "would be in our reconciliation bill," referring to a measure Congress has put on a fast track in order to repeal major pieces of the health law.

But just as Republicans are discovering that undoing the health law could be complicated, so too is separating the controversial reproductive health care provider from its federal funding. Efforts to hastily jettison Planned Parenthood from federal ledgers could actually jeopardize GOP efforts to repeal the health law.

One problem is that Planned Parenthood gets its funding from several different government sources. According to the group's most recent annual report, Planned Parenthood affiliates got $553.7 million from federal, state, and local governments, accounting for almost half of its total funding.

According to the organization, about 75 percent of that government support comes from the Medicaid program to pay for direct medical services provided to low-income patients, including contraception, cancer screenings and sexually transmitted disease testing and treatment. The remaining quarter comes from other sources, primarily the Title X federal family planning program. The Congressional Budget Office estimated last year that the group gets approximately $390 million annually from Medicaid and $60 million from Title X.

None of the funds from either program may be used for abortion, under longstanding federal prohibitions. Only half of the Planned Parenthood affiliates even offer abortion services, the group says. But it is still the largest single provider of the procedure in the nation, and that has made it a target for anti-abortion lawmakers since the 1980s.

In recent years, one of the most ardent foes of the organization has been Vice President-elect Mike Pence. When he was a member of the House of Representatives, he led unsuccessful efforts to defund the program. As governor of Indiana, he was able to accomplish some of his goals. He also vowed to stop federal spending for Planned Parenthood during the campaign last fall.

Yet federal lawmakers have been stymied in these efforts.

One big reason is that taking away Planned Parenthood's access to Medicaid funding would require a change in the federal law that guarantees most Medicaid patients with a choice to use any qualified provider. The Department of Health and Human Services has repeatedly warned states that have tried to evict Planned Parenthood from their Medicaid programs that they cannot legally do that because such a move would violate that law. And federal courts have consistently blocked states that have tried to end Planned Parenthood's Medicaid funding.

Changing that section of Medicaid law likely would require 60 votes in the Senate to break a filibuster by Democrats. Republicans currently have 52 votes. However, the budget reconciliation bill that is expected to be used to repeal portions of the health law operates under special rules. It cannot be filibustered and needs only 51 votes to pass.

That presents two problems for Republicans.

According to a 2015 Congressional Budget Office analysis, permanently changing the Medicaid law to make Planned Parenthood ineligible would cost more, not less—approximately $130 million over 10 years. That is because, said the Congressional Budget Office, taking away contraceptive access for some women would result in more pregnancies, and "additional births that would result from enacting such a bill would add to federal spending for Medicaid."

That is not just theoretical. In 2013, Texas kicked Planned Parenthood out of its family planning program and gave up its federal funding. The result was fewer women using birth control and more babies being born, according to an analysis published last March in *The New England Journal of Medicine*.

The second problem is political. While the House under GOP control has been strongly in favor of cutting off Planned Parenthood's access to federal funds, there are a handful of Republican senators who oppose the idea. And a handful—three, to be exact—is all it would take to threaten passage of the health law repeal effort.

"Obviously I'm not happy that the speaker has decided to include the defunding of Planned Parenthood—an extremely controversial issue—in the (budget reconciliation) package," Sen. Susan Collins, R-Maine, told reporters earlier this month.

A spokeswoman for Sen. Lisa Murkowski, R-Alaska, said "she is concerned about defunding Planned Parenthood, as she is a longtime supporter of Planned Parenthood and has opposed broadly defunding the organization."

Collins and Murkowski fought against the inclusion of a one-year defunding of the organization in a 2015 health law repeal bill that President Obama vetoed last January.

Although neither senator has said she would vote against the upcoming budget bill if it includes the Planned Parenthood defunding, they join a growing list of Senate Republicans who in recent days have questioned the idea of repealing major portions of the health law before devising its replacement.

Meanwhile, eliminating Planned Parenthood's access to funding under Title X also would likely be addressed in an appropriations spending bill. The current spending bill for the Department of Health and Human Services (and most of the rest of the government) expires April 28.

But rather than simply making Planned Parenthood ineligible, Republicans in the House have proposed doing away with funding for the entire 45-year-old Title X federal family planning program. Instead, they would send the money to the nation's network of community health centers.

Last September, the Trump-Pence campaign released a letter to anti-abortion leaders vowing to defund Planned Parenthood "as long as they continue to perform abortions, and reallocating their funding to community health centers that provide comprehensive health care for women."

At a CNN town hall Thursday night, Ryan expanded on that. "We don't want to effectively commit taxpayer money to an organization providing abortions. But we want to make sure that people get their coverage. That's why there's no conflict by making sure these dollars go to federal community health centers."

But that might not work either.

"For health centers, which currently serve about 25 million total patients, to have to absorb an additional 2 million people is totally impossible," says Sara Rosenbaum, a health policy and law professor at George Washington University who looked at the issue in 2015.

In some areas of the country, Planned Parenthood and community health centers may not overlap. Planned Parenthood says that in a fifth of the counties it serves, it is the only provider for low-income women. Asking community health centers to move into new areas, says Rosenbaum, "displays a fundamental misunderstanding of how long it takes a new provider to move into a potentially new community."

Despite the difficulties, the shifts in political control this year leaves Planned Parenthood concerned about its future.

While the organization has weathered funding threats before, "it is very true when you have people like Mike Pence and Paul Ryan who have been laser focused for years [on ending funding], that they will make it a very high priority," says Mary Alice Carter, Planned Parenthood's vice president for communications.

She says the organization is counting on the 2.5 million patients it serves every year to make sure their elected officials know they oppose the defunding effort. Whether that will be enough remains unclear.

8

Women's Health Care in Jeopardy Under New Administration

Jamila Taylor

Political scientist Jamila K. Taylor is a senior fellow at American Progress, where she serves as an expert on domestic and international women's health, reproductive rights, and reproductive justice.

In the following viewpoint, Jamila Taylor warns that Congressional Republicans and the Trump-Pence administration are both taking aim at women's reproductive rights. Defunding Planned Parenthood and repealing the ACA are the two primary means to this end. The ACA has greatly expanded women's access to insurance and preventative services such as annual exams and screenings. The ACA also mandates full contraception coverage, saving women $1.4 billion. Planned Parenthood has been a longstanding crucial resource and safety net, particularly for low-income women. Attacks on these institutions will negatively impact women's physical and economic well-being.

Congressional Republicans and the incoming Trump-Pence administration have a loathsome preoccupation with crippling access to women's health care. Notable efforts at the core of their anti-choice/anti-woman agenda are defunding Planned Parenthood and repealing the Affordable Care Act, or ACA. These efforts are front and center in current negotiations around the annual

"How Women Would Be Hurt by ACA Repeal and Defunding of Planned Parenthood," by Jamila Taylor, Center for American Progress, January 18, 2017. Reprinted by Permission.

budget reconciliation bill and ensuing confirmation hearings for key political appointees, including Rep. Tom Price (R-GA) for health and human services secretary and Sen. Jeff Sessions (R-AL) for attorney general. Both men are on record supporting legislation to derail access to women's health care. If congressional Republicans succeed in repealing the ACA and defunding Planned Parenthood, women would be tremendously disadvantaged by the loss of affordable health care.

The ACA Significantly Expanded Affordable Health Care Coverage for Women

The ACA has helped ensure access to quality, affordable care for millions of women. Approximately 9.5 million women who were previously uninsured have gained health coverage through the ACA; 55 million women now have access to vital preventive care at no cost. Some of the covered preventive services include annual well-woman exams; breast-feeding support and supplies for new moms; birth control; screening and counseling for domestic and intimate partner violence; and screening and treatment for sexually transmitted infections. Such services provide critical, holistic care for women who previously struggled to meet these needs due to cost and lack of access.

One of the most popular aspects in the suite of ACA-mandated services is the requirement that all contraceptive methods approved by the U.S. Federal Drug Administration must be covered by insurance without cost sharing. A University of Michigan Health System poll found that nearly 7 in 10 Americans support this mandate. This benefit alone has saved women $1.4 billion in out-of-pocket costs each year since going into effect in 2012.

Additional supports for women's health that are built into the ACA include the requirement that all small group and individual health plans provide coverage for maternity care. Furthermore, women can no longer be charged more for their health insurance or be denied coverage due to pre-existing conditions. And young women can stay on their parent's insurance plans until age 26. The

ACA also made it illegal for government agencies and federally funded health insurers and hospitals to discriminate based on sex, race, color, national origin, disability or age. This is the first time federal civil rights law has prohibited discrimination based on sex in federally funded health programs.

Significantly, the ACA provides women with benefits that go beyond physical health. When a woman doesn't have to pay a $20 copay for a well-woman visit or $1,000 for an intrauterine device, or IUD, she can save that money or use it for household expenses. Countless studies have shown that health care costs are a barrier for women seeking health services. If the ACA is repealed, women's insurance rates will increase because their health services are more expensive and women could be denied health coverage due to pre-existing conditions.

ACA repeal and the ensuing rollback of Medicaid expansion would drag the country back to a time when some women and families were forced to go without health insurance. Loss of vital services such as free birth control, maternity care, and preventive services will hit women of color and low-income women hardest—contributing to health inequity and health disparities. And if congressional Republicans defund Planned Parenthood in addition to repealing the ACA, they will push sexual and reproductive health care even farther out of reach for communities in need.

Defunding Planned Parenthood Would Bar Access to Health Care Through the Safety Net

Planned Parenthood has been a leader in providing health services to communities for 100 years. The organization currently operates 650 health centers throughout the country. Comprehensive sexual and reproductive health care is a part of Planned Parenthood's DNA; often it is the sole source of family planning for many of the women it serves. Planned Parenthood clinics provide breast cancer screenings; testing and treatment for sexually transmitted infections; pap tests; cervical cancer screenings; family planning and birth control counseling and services; sexuality education and outreach; and more.

While Republicans have attacked Planned Parenthood for offering abortion services, abortion is an essential aspect in the continuum of sexual and reproductive health care and accounts for only about 3 percent of the services the organization provides. Nearly 5 million women, men, and adolescents are served by Planned Parenthood each year. One in five women in the United States will visit a Planned Parenthood health center at least once in her lifetime.

Withholding federal funding from Planned Parenthood would have a significant impact on the organization's ability to provide much-needed services. In 2014, the organization's total revenue was about $1.3 billion, with $533 million from the federal government. Planned Parenthood receives federal funds primarily through the Title X family planning program and Medicaid reimbursements. These funds are subject to the draconian restriction on federal funding for abortion, known as the Hyde Amendment. Nearly two-thirds of Planned Parenthood patients access their care through federally funded health programs. Because Planned Parenthood largely serves low-income women, women of color, young women, and immigrant women, these communities stand to face the worst health and economic outcomes if this safety net provider is blocked from receiving federal funds. Oftentimes, Planned Parenthood is the single access point of primary care for many of its patients, including women on Medicaid and the uninsured.

Conclusion

Reproductive freedom and sustained physical health are integral to women's ability to remain productive and contribute to their own and their families' wellbeing. Repealing the ACA and defunding Planned Parenthood would not only jeopardize many women's physical health, but their economic security would also take a hit if they are forced to assume increased health care costs. The incoming Trump-Pence administration and anti-choice members of Congress are out of touch with what women need to lead healthy, productive lives that allow them to play a vital role in sustaining the nation's communities. Women's health care should not be a political wedge issue.

9

Women's March Draws Thousands but Exposes Racial Fissures

Karen Grigsby Bates

Karen Grigsby Bates is a Los Angeles–based correspondent for NPR News. Bates contributed commentaries to All Things Considered *for about ten years before she joined NPR in 2002 as the first correspondent and alternate host for* The Tavis Smiley Show.

In this viewpoint, Karen Grigsby Bates links the January 2017 Women's March on Washington to longstanding race and class-based tensions within the feminist movement. For decades, women of color argued that feminism spoke mainly to and for middle and upper class white women, while marginalizing women who did not fit this description. Some have even rejected the term "feminism" for this reason. Despite calls for unity in the Trump era, these concerns need to be addressed. White middle and upper class women need to speak less and listen more in order to ally themselves with this goal.

The streets of Washington looked vastly different the day after Donald J. Trump's inauguration than they did the day-of. Instead of the largely white crowds that lined Pennsylvania Avenue on Inauguration Day, people of all colors, classes and ages filled the streets for what's being called the most diverse march for women's rights ever.

The Women's March on Washington drew tens of thousands to the nation's capital to press for protection of women's rights, including reproductive health care, LGBT issues and equal pay. "Sister marches" held concurrently in every state across the nation (and in several cities abroad) added to the numbers and the diversity.

But all that diversity came with a cost: racial tension—not just around the march itself, but around the feminist movement, who leads it and why. Some bemoaned the discord as a distraction from the march, saying on this occasion, "we should all be women first."

Grace Hong is not surprised. A professor of Asian American and Gender Studies at UCLA, Hong says for decades, white women didn't have to consider any interests beyond their own because "historically, the category 'woman' has, implicitly, meant *white* women." The call to put womanhood above all else, Hong says, is based on the idea that "critique and dissent undermine a unity that's based on the lowest common denominator: Find the one thing everyone has in common."

The fact that the feminist movement was so white for so long, says Ashley Farmer, is the reason so many women of color steered clear of it. Farmer is a historian at Boston University, and concentrates on African-American women's history. She says women of color noticed when their interests and needs didn't get a full hearing.

"When we actually get down to representation or creating a list of demands or mobilizing around a set of ideas," Farmer says, "it tends to be that white middle-class or upper-class women's priorities get put above the rest."

It was that way in the 1850s, when some feminists split over whether to champion abolition or women's rights. (That's when Sojourner Truth gave her famous "Ain't I A Woman?" speech at a women's rights conference in Ohio.)

It was that way in the late '60s and early '70s, when "Sisterhood is Powerful" became a rallying cry—but with very few exceptions

(Flo Kennedy, Shirley Chisholm, Eleanor Holmes Norton) brown and black sisters were very much on the sidelines. It's why some African-American women, like writers Alice Walker and bell hooks, chose to refer to themselves as "womanist," not feminist. They refused to divorce their race from their gender. (They were intersectional before intersectionality as a term came into existence, created by black feminist legal scholar Kimberlé Crenshaw.)

Today, "womanist" also resonates with a younger generation of feminists, not all of them black. Dolores Arredondo, a marketing executive with Wells Fargo, in Los Angeles, has been calling herself a womanist for years, in direct response to what she saw as white feminists' exclusion. "I just remember this history of the feminist movement," Arredondo shrugs. "I can see the history, and none of them looked like me." Arredondo attended the Los Angeles march with her 13-year-old daughter Sophie.

Brenda Gonzales-Richards says she's not hung up on labels. The director of the California regional office for the National Council of La Raza, a Latino civil rights group, Gonzales-Richards says she'll answer to most anything—feminist, womanist, whatever—but she has another term she prefers: *chingona.*

"It means badass!" she says, gleefully. "A chingona is someone who is not afraid to stand up for what they believe in, somebody that's happy to shake things up when needed." Chingonas, she says, get things done. And they come in all races and genders.

The Women's March on Washington started out pretty white, but quickly added young women of color in positions of leadership. They're three of the four main organizers, and a lot of attention has been paid to how diverse this march has been in contrast to earlier ones. But even as the march's diversity was being celebrated, it was also causing tension.

When ShiShi Rose, a young black Brooklyn blogger, wrote an Instagram post advising white women allies that "now is the time for you to be listening more, talking less." She suggested they become more conversant in culture beyond the mainstream standard. Some white women were so offended that they cancelled plans to attend the march.

Margo Jefferson doesn't have much patience with that. A Pulitzer Prize-winning cultural critic for *The New York Times* for years (and part of the Artist Table of creatives and celebrities who participated in the New York sister march), Jefferson remembers being one the few early black feminists who called themselves that. ("Of *course* I was lonely back then," she admits. "It was harder for black women to make a feminist movement in the 1970s.")

Jefferson advises white women who were offended by Rose's post to "Sit back. You're associated with a history that has to do with being bossy and self-absorbed and bigoted in some ways. I can see how that would rattle, and even anger you," she says gently. "But I do not consider it reason enough to cancel an attendance at a march like this. Get over it."

Julie Wittes Schlack is a Boston writer and corporate executive who was neither rattled nor offended by criticism from women of color. If the movement is going to progress to the next level, Schlack believes, white feminists like her are going to have to deal with some hard truths. They are right to be proud of their contributions to women's progress in this country, she says, but more needs to be done.

"The benefits of our work so far around things like reproductive rights aren't conferred equally across all women," Schlack points out. "And that's what I think younger feminists, feminists of color, particularly, are trying to wake us up to." The issues are broader, messier, more intersectional: race, gender, class, nationality, immigration status, everything is connected.

The wake-up Schlack refers to won't just benefit women of color, points out Boston University's Ashley Farmer: "When you make something that accounts for the most oppressed, everybody's life tends to get better."

But that process may have bumps from time to time. UCLA's Grace Hong believes the discord around today's marches may, in the end, be good for feminism: "Maybe the point is to *not* all agree," she says. "Maybe the point is to do these kinds of things so that you can have the tough conversations."

And maybe, she says, these marches are the next step toward having those tough, but necessary, talks.

10

Why We Need Intersectional Feminism

Taylor Hawk

Taylor Hawk is a contributor to Denison University's Women and Gender Studies blog, as well as the blogging platform Odyssey, and is a member of the university's class of 2020.

In the following viewpoint, Taylor Hawk explains intersectional feminism and underscores its importance. Professor and activist Kimberlé Crenshaw invented the term, but it has since become a buzzword with a reach expanding far beyond the confines of academic theory. According to Hawk, intersectional feminism is needed to redress an inherent bias within feminism toward the experience of white women. By taking into account how race and class also determine women's experience, intersectional theory resists the totalizing, universalizing impulses of past iterations of the feminist movement that focused on improving lives for those already of some privilege.

Most know that feminism is the movement set on achieving gender equality. But not as many know what intersectional feminism is.

So what is it, exactly? The term intersectionality was coined by civil rights activist and professor Kimberlé Crenshaw and can be defined as "the interconnected nature of social categorizations such as race, class, and gender as they apply to a given individual

"What Is 'Intersectional Feminism'?" by Taylor Hawk, Denison University, July 26, 2016. Reprinted by Permission. Odyssey Online.

or group, regarded as creating overlapping and interdependent systems of discrimination or disadvantage." By adding the idea of intersectionality to feminism, the movement becomes truly inclusive and allows women of all races, economic standings, religions, identities and orientations for their voices to be heard.

Over the course of its existence, feminism has mainly focused on the issues experienced by white, middle-class women. For example, it is largely shared and advertised that a woman makes 78 cents to a man's dollar. But this is only the statistic for white women. As upsetting as it is, women of minority groups make even less. Black women earn 64 cents to white men's dollar and Hispanic women only earn 56 cents. Intersectional feminism takes into account the many different ways each woman experiences discrimination. "White feminism" is a term that is used to describe a type of feminism that overshadows the struggles women of color, LGBTQ women and women of other minority groups face. So, essentially, it's not true feminism at all.

[…]"White feminism" ignores intersectionality and neglects to recognize the discriminations experienced by women who are not white. It's important to note that not all feminists who are white practice "white feminism." "White feminism" depicts the way white women face gender inequality as the way all women experience gender inequality, which just isn't correct.

Unfortunately, celebrities and the media are often guilty of doing this as well. An example of this is the great Nicki Minaj and Taylor Swift debacle of 2015. As Nicki tweeted her disappointment of not being nominated for Video of The Year, she brought to light a very important issue. She pointed out that most music videos nominated only showed white, slender-bodied women. Taylor took this as a personal dig and sent out the now infamous tweet in response. Instead of using her voice to recognize the prevalent problem Nicki was discussing, Taylor became defensive and claimed Nicki was pitting women against women. Eventually, the "feud" came to an end when Nicki had Taylor join her onstage for her performance. But, this exchange can still serve as a reminder of how important intersectionality really is.

The key to combating "white feminism" is education about intersectionality. In an interview, Crenshaw defines intersectionality as, "the idea that we experience life, sometimes discrimination, sometimes benefits, based on a number of identities." She first started to develop her theory on intersectionality when she studied the ways black women are discriminated against for both their gender and race. She comments, "The basic term came out of a case where I was looking at black women who were being discriminated against, not just as black people and not just as women, but as black women. So, intersectionality was basically just a metaphor to say they are facing race discrimination from one direction. They have gender discrimination from another direction, and they're colliding in their li ves in ways we really don't anticipate and understand."

So, now that we understand what intersectionality is, how can we incorporate it into our feminism? As explained by Laci Green and Franchesca Ramsey, two awesome Internet ladies,...there can be three easy steps in achieving intersectional feminism. They explain the steps as, "1. Examine our own privilege. 2. Listen to each other. 3. Practice feminism through a broader, more inclusive lens."

It's crucial to check your own privilege in society in order to be a better feminist. I, for example, am a white, straight, able-bodied, middle-class woman. This means that I personally don't have to face challenges that other women do. So, it's important that I recognize my privilege and listen to women who experience the world differently than I do. As Laci says in the video, "On the feminist issues where we hold privilege, it's crucial to listen to women who don't. To listen to their experiences, to see the world through a more complex lens and to raise the voices of those who have less power." Franchesca adds, "You can't exactly walk the walk if you have no idea where the walk even goes." Despite how daunting and intimidating the term intersectionality may seem, it's just about us standing up and looking out for each other.

Intersectionality is a term used to describe how different factors of discrimination can meet at an intersection and can affect someone's life. Adding intersectionality to feminism is important to the movement because it allows the fight for gender equality to become inclusive. Using intersectionality allows us all to understand each other a little bit better.

At the end of the day, we might all experience discrimination and gender inequality differently and uniquely, but we are all united in our hope for equality.

11

Women Worldwide Will Suffer Under Global Gag Rule

Jamila Taylor and Kiersten Gillette-Pierce

Jamila K. Taylor is a senior fellow at American Progress, where she serves as an expert on domestic and international women's health, reproductive rights, and reproductive justice, and Kiersten Gillette-Pierce is a 2017–2019 Peace Corps extension volunteer, specializing in maternal and child health.

In the following viewpoint, Jamila Taylor and Kiersten Gillette-Pierce discuss the Mexico City Policy, more commonly known as the Global Gag Rule. The policy forbids recipients of US foreign aid from earmarking money for abortion-related services. Observers predict the Trump administration will reinstate this policy through an executive action. If this occurs, unintended pregnancies, unsafe abortions, and maternal deaths will surely increase for women worldwide, particularly in the developing world. The Global Gag Rule diminishes women's autonomy and bars access to family planning information as well as contraception. It is economically costly and, worse still, will cause women to suffer unnecessarily.

President Donald Trump is likely to follow the tradition of other Republican anti-choice administrations and reinstate the Mexico City Policy, which bans recipients of U.S. foreign aid from offering abortion-related services, as one of his first executive

"What's at Stake for Women: Threat of the Global Gag Rule," by Jamila Taylor and Kiersten Gillette-Pierce, Center for American Progress, January 23, 2017. Reprinted by Permission.

actions. Better known as the Global Gag Rule and first introduced in 1984 at the U.N. International Conference on Population held in Mexico City, the policy has been a barrier to comprehensive women's health care on a global scale.[1] Made U.S. policy through an executive order issued by President Ronald Reagan, it restricts family planning providers from offering comprehensive health care and, when in place, denies international family planning organizations the right to:[2]

- Provide abortion-related information to their patients and clients[3]
- Provide referrals to other health care providers who perform safe abortions[4]
- Provide legal abortions or legal abortion-related services[5]
- Advocate for the legalization of abortion in their country[6]

The Mexico City Policy infringes upon women's fundamental right to make informed decisions about their bodies and their health. It denies women access to comprehensive sexual and reproductive health care that includes abortion care and related information and referrals.

When former President Barack Obama assumed office in 2009, one of the first executive actions he took was to revoke the ban, which had been reinstated after George W. Bush came into office in 2001 following the Clinton administration. The end of the Obama administration brings to the forefront just how much is at stake for women if the Global Gag Rule is reinstated. Historically under Republican administrations, the policy has imposed barriers on any organization receiving U.S.[7] international family planning funding. The policy is put into place via executive order; thus, presidential administrations can dictate family planning measures depending upon whether they support reproductive choice.

This makes continuing the promotion of technical assistance to recipient countries and contraception access difficult. Shortly after the reinstatement of the Mexico City Policy in 2001, for example, shipments of donated contraceptives—including condoms—were completely stopped from the United States.[8] This left 20 developing countries without much-needed contraceptive supplies. In addition, a 2011 Stanford University study found that organizations that refused to sign the Global Gag Rule completely lost U.S. Agency for International Development, or USAID, funding.[9] As a result, abortion rates increased in countries where these organizations were working to more than twice the rate prior to the presidency of George W. Bush.[10]

The Global Gag Rule directly affects access to women's health care in U.S.-funded global health programs overseas, as well as the providers themselves by forcing them to decide between U.S. aid for family assistance and providing comprehensive, modern care.

The Global Gag Rule puts undue burden on U.S.-funded health care providers and women seeking their services

Since 1973, the Helms Amendment has restricted the use of U.S. foreign assistance funds for the performance of abortion "as a method of family planning."[11] It is a restriction that is statute and applied to all U.S. foreign assistance funding. The Global Gag Rule, on the other hand, is put into place via executive order and restricts international family planning funding only—barring U.S.-funded health care providers who work overseas from even using their own private funds to engage in any work related to abortion.[12] Moreover, without the free speech protections afforded to U.S. organizations through the Constitution, the Global Gag Rule is used as a political football that is solely dependent upon the presidential administration's views on abortion. This means that whoever holds the office of the president dictates the right of women overseas to access comprehensive sexual and reproductive health care. The policy has also done great harm to health care providers by making the provision of comprehensive health care for women an unnecessarily burdensome task.

If a provider refuses to sign the Global Gag Rule, it loses:

- U.S. funding[13]
- Donated contraceptives—including condoms[14]
- Cutting-edge leadership and technical expertise, which is predominantly provided by the U.S. international family planning program within USAID[15]

In the past, the abrupt cutting of funds has led to entire health care networks collapsing, with providers noting a lack of resources and resorting to higher service costs in order to maintain efficiency.[16]

If a provider agrees to sign the Global Gag Rule, it must comply with strict guidelines.[17] To secure USAID family planning funds, organizations often forfeit free speech and control of their services.[18] For example, providers under the Global Gag Rule lose critical rights such as the ability to practice full consent—independent decision-making between doctor and patient.[19] Without the right to disseminate abortion-related information, the patient-provider relationship is strained. Fearing reprimand, international family planning providers sacrifice critical, often lifesaving advice. Even permitted services, such as treatment for injuries due to unsafe abortion, are at times inaccessible to women because providers refuse to risk viable funding.

Women globally deserve the right to autonomy and comprehensive care

The Global Gag Rule is also a barrier to addressing other global health priorities such as HIV/AIDS prevention and maternal and child health. International family planning providers have the expertise and resources to advise patients about risky behaviors and safer sex practices and to screen for and treat sexually transmitted infections, or STIs, including HIV.[20] However, when the Global Gag Rule is in place, health care providers who address global health priorities and work with at-risk populations—namely, women, young people, and those who disagree with the policy—are often unable to engage in important partnerships with the United States.

Moreover, the loss of U.S. funding contributes to the unmet need for modern contraception for more than 225 million women globally.[21] Access to contraception is vital to the success of women, children, and their communities. By empowering women with proper health care access, their ability to help build their nations' economies is bolstered. When given full access to U.S. international family planning funding and assistance, health care providers would be better able to help women in developing nations have safe pregnancies, avoid unsafe abortion, and have access to contraceptives. Without the burden of the Mexico City Policy, women and their health care providers have the ability to engage in autonomous, comprehensive, and life-altering care.

In the absence of the Mexico City Policy, health care providers have the ability to establish open communication with women about their family planning and overall health options. A healthy patient-provider relationship and access to U.S. governmental funds, void of draconian restrictions, means tangible change for women's health outcomes and implements autonomous comprehensive care. Some of the key health outcomes yielded by having access to family planning services include:

- Increasing the likelihood that more women gain needed access to other facets of the health care system[22]
- Decreasing women's likelihood of attaining an unsafe abortion or dying from pregnancy-related complications[23]
- Sparing 8.4 million women from serious illness or injury from unsafe abortion complications[24]
- Saving an estimated 289,000 women from pregnancy- or childbirth-related deaths[25]
- Providing an estimated 50,000 adolescent mothers and more than 1 million infants a chance at life via measures such as contraceptives, prenatal care, and postnatal care[26]
- Ensuring that 75 percent of sexually active adolescents in developing countries have access to contraceptives[27]

For all women and girls, the Global Gag Rule is a breach of autonomy. By taking away family planning and stigmatizing abortion, the United States is withholding women's human right to safe and informed sexual health; reliable STI/HIV treatment; safe abortion care; safe pregnancies and childbirth; and ultimately, their ability to make substantial contributions to their communities.

Action against the Global Gag Rule under the Trump administration

If President Trump reinstates the Global Gag Rule, the global community will see increases in maternal deaths, unintended pregnancies, and rates of unsafe abortion. As the world's largest bilateral donor of international family planning, the United States is obligated to do better by the nations it serves.[28] The Global Democracy Promotion Act—legislation aimed at ensuring that international family planning will not be inhibited by undue governmental interference—is a first step in that direction.[29]

This act would end the case of ineligibility for U.S. foreign aid recipients due to use of nongovernmental funds for provider-specified services, such as abortion or abortion-related care. It would also help keep U.S. presidents from unilaterally imposing the Global Gag Rule and chipping away at the human rights of women overseas. Congress must make concerted efforts to reintroduce, and ultimately pass, this bill because women and girls deserve to freely make decisions about their sexual and reproductive health.

Endnotes

1. Ipas, "The Global Gag Rule harms democracy, women and U.S. interests abroad" (2007), available at http://www.ipas.org/en/Resources/Ipas%20Publications/The-Global-Gag-Rule-harms-democracy-women-and-US.aspx.

2. NARAL Pro-Choice America, "Global Gag Rule: A Flawed Policy That Sacrifices Women's Lives" (2016), available at http://www.prochoiceamerica.org/media/fact-sheets/abortion-funding-global-gag.pdf.

3. Ibid.

4. Ibid.

5. Ibid.

6. Ibid.

7. Population Connection and NARAL Pro-Choice America, "Effects of the Global Gag Rule: Examples from Around the World" (2016), available at http://www .prochoiceamerica.org/media/fact-sheets/abortion-funding-effects-of-the-global -gag.pdf.

8. PAI, "How the Global Gag Rule Undermines U.S. Foreign Policy and Harms Women's Health" (2015), available at http://pai.org/gag-rule/img/PAI-Gag-PIB.pdf.

9. Eran Bendavid, Patrick Avila, and Grant Miller, "United States aid policy and induced abortion in sub-Saharan Africa," *Bulletin of the World Health Organization* 89 (2011): 873–880, available at http://www.scielosp.org/pdf/bwho/v89n12 /a10v89n12.pdf.

10. Ibid.

11. Jamila Taylor, "How U.S. Foreign Policy Blocks Women's Access to Safe Abortion Overseas" (Chapel Hill, NC: Ipas, 2013), available at http://www.ipas.org/en /Resources/Ipas%20Publications/How-U-S–Foreign-Policy-Blocks-Women-s -Access-to-Safe-Abortion-Overseas.aspx.

12. Ipas, "The Global Gag Rule harms democracy, women and U.S. interests abroad."

13. Population Connection and NARAL Pro-Choice America, "Effects of the Global Gag Rule."

14. PAI, "How the Global Gag Rule Undermines U.S. Foreign Policy and Harms Women's Health."

15. Ibid.

16. Ibid.

17. NARAL Pro-Choice America, "Global Gag Rule: A Flawed Policy That Sacrifices Women's Lives."

18. PAI, "How the Global Gag Rule Undermines U.S. Foreign Policy and Harms Women's Health."

19. Ibid.

20. Ibid.

21. Ibid.

22. Ibid.

23. Ibid.

24. Ibid.

25. World Health Organization, "Maternal Mortality," available at http://www.who.int /mediacentre/factsheets/fs348/en/ (last accessed January 2017).

26. Kathryn Rawe and others, "Every Woman's Right: How family planning saves children's lives" (London: Save the Children, 2012), available at http://www .savethechildren.org/atf/cf/%7B9def2ebe-10ae-432c-9bd0-df91d2eba74a%7D /EVERY_WOMANS_RIGHT_REPORT_JUNE_2012.PDF.

27. Ann K. Blanc and others, "Patterns and Trends in Adolescents' Contraceptive Use and Discontinuation in Developing Countries and Comparisons with Adult Women," *International Perspectives on Sexual and Reproductive Health* 35 (2) (2009): 63–71, available at https://www.guttmacher.org/sites/default/files/article_ files/3506309.pdf.

28. Planned Parenthood Action Fund, "End the Global Gag Rule," available at https://www.plannedparenthoodaction.org/communities/planned-parenthood-global/end-global-gag-rule (last accessed January 2017).

29. *Global Democracy Promotion Act*, H. Rept. 2740, 114 Cong. 1 sess. (Government Printing Office, 2015).

12

Global Gag Rule Defunds Aid to the Poor

Patricia Schwerdtle

Patricia Schwerdtle is a global health and nursing academic based at Monash University.

In the following viewpoint, Patricia Schwerdtle elaborates on the destructive effects the Global Gag Rule will have on the world's poor and vulnerable populations, particularly women in the developing world. Western European governments are pledging millions to make up for the funding shortfall the conservative turn in US policy has imposed. Providing access to contraception takes time and money. Moreover, studies have shown that the Global Gag Rule has increased abortions, and women in impoverished areas are almost three times as likely to have an abortion under the rule than without it. Any rational assessment of public health reveals that the Global Gag Rule is ineffective policy.

Two days after large numbers of people across the globe joined Woman's Marches, US President Donald Trump reinstated the "global gag rule," which cuts off all US funding to international NGOs whose work includes abortion services or advocacy.

Fortunately, the Dutch government has announced a plan to compensate NGOs for the funding shortfall of US$600 million

"Trump's 'Global Gag Rule' Will Cause More Abortions, Not Fewer," by Patricia Schwerdtle, The Conversation, January 26, 2017. https://theconversation.com/trumps-global-gag-rule-will-cause-more-abortions-not-fewer-71881. Licensed Under CC BY-ND 4.0 International.

over four years. Several countries within and outside the EU have indicated their support, as have private companies and foundations.

But it remains to be seen whether this ambitious target will be reached and what other needs will be left unmet as a result of any redirected funds.

Dutch Minister for International Development Co-operation, Lilianne Ploumen, who announced the initiative, said, "I'm pro-choice and pro-women's rights. It's important to stand your ground."

But as welcome as efforts towards replacing the funding lost to the global gag rule is, it's important to realise that this is not a pro-life debate. It's a global health issue that has serious implications for the most vulnerable populations—millions of men, women and children in developing countries.

Threat to Services

Also known as the Mexico City policy, the global gag rule requires all NGOs operating abroad to refrain from advising, endorsing or performing abortions as a method of family planning. However, some NGOs operate in contexts where abortion—safe or unsafe—is the only accessible form of contraception.

Many international NGOs are working hard to increase access to both short-term and long-term contraception. But such a transition takes time and money.

NGOs that may be forced to reduce or close health services as a result of the policy are often a woman's only source of reproductive health care. They may, in fact, be her family's only point of medical contact for other primary health-care services, such as cervical screening, HIV prevention, testing and counselling, STI prevention and treatment, pre and post-natal care and even newborn health care.

Services threatened by the policy also train health professionals, including midwives and traditional birth attendants, in countries that are desperately short of qualified health personnel.

Most developed countries have 33 health professionals per 10,000 people; most developing countries have two health professionals for the same number of people. Research also shows that unattended births have much higher rates of maternal and newborn death.

Unintended Consequences

The rule was first put into place by former US president Ronald Reagan in August 1984. Since then, it has been lifted by Democratic presidents and reinstated by Republican presidents.

Unlike when Reagan implemented the policy, we now have ample evidence of its unintended health consequences. A 2011 study showed, that women were 2.73 times more likely to have an abortion under the rule. So while its intention may be to reduce the rate of abortion, the policy actually increases it.

Reducing access to family planning services leads to more unplanned pregnancies, more unsafe abortions and more maternal death.

The sexual and reproductive health research organisation, the Guttmacher Institute, quantified this in 2016. It showed that when US$607.5 million is cut from family planning and reproductive health services, 27 million women and couples are prevented from receiving family planning services and supplies. This leads to six million more unplanned pregnancies and 2.3 million more abortions, two million of which will be unsafe.

This may not mean much in a developed country, where deaths resulting from pregnancy and childbirth are 12 women per 100,000 live births. But it will have a huge impact on women in developing countries, where the maternal mortality rate is 239 women per 100,000 live births, and where 99% of total global maternal deaths occur.

In 2000, 189 countries, including the United States, committed to the Millennium Development Goals. These included a commitment to improving maternal health by reducing maternal mortality and providing access to reproductive health services by 2015. This was one of the least successful Millennium Development Goals, falling short by half.

Falling Short

While the US ranks 19th worldwide as an international aid donor in terms of percentage of gross national income, USAID is the largest humanitarian donor in dollar terms. It allocated in excess of $USD6.42 billion to humanitarian aid in 2015.

This means the global gag rule seriously threatens the UN Sustainable Development Goal of reducing maternal mortality to less than 70 per 100,000 live births by 2030. It also threatens the goal of ensuring access to sexual and reproductive health-care services, including family planning, information and education.

The rule targets family planning, which is essentially about spacing out childbirth. The health and economic benefits of child spacing are well documented and include reduced pregnancy-related deaths and better child survival. Then, there's reduced rates of HIV/AIDS, and sexually transmitted infections, empowerment of women, enhanced education and a reduction in adolescent pregnancy.

These benefits lead to more advantages, including slowed population growth, natural resource conservation, climate change mitigation and economic growth, which reduces conflict and migration.

The Wrong Debate

Forcing impoverished women—in places where they have no access to health care or contraception—to have more babies has a detrimental impact on the entire family. It places demands on scarce resources, reduces access to education, limits employment options, reduces family income and ultimately reinforces the poverty cycle.

The regions predicted to experience the largest population growth in the coming decades (South Asia and Africa) are also the most impoverished. They have the weakest health-care systems and rely on foreign aid to provide essential services.

Their only hope for economic development and poverty eradication is to undergo the demographic transition, which high-income countries have already experienced. And this starts with a reduction in family size. Anyone who has worked in reproductive health in developing countries will tell you that this is what impoverished women with large families want.

So let's get it right: this is not a high-income country, religiously charged pro-life debate. The global gag rule actually increases abortion demand and has consequences for a range of other health issues such as HIV/AIDS, cervical cancer and child health and well-being.

This misinformed, short-sighted policy is as far removed from scientific evidence as denying climate change. As a global community, we have a duty to expand access to family planning for people worldwide, particularly to the most vulnerable.

13

US Paid Leave Policies Lag Behind Those of Other Democracies

Danielle Kurtzleben

Danielle Kurtzleben is a political reporter assigned to NPR's Washington desk. At present, she writes for NPR's It's All Politics blog. She has also worked for Vox Media and U.S. News & World Report.

In this viewpoint, Danielle Kurtzleben compares US work leave policies to those of other nations. Out of all the Organization for Economic Cooperation and Development (OECD) member countries, the United States is the only one that does not mandate some form of paid maternity leave. We are also one of only nine countries that deny fathers paid paternity leave. President Obama tried to bring attention to the issue of paid parental and sick leave. Likewise, Hillary Clinton advocated for more lenient policies, but her presidential loss indicates that reform on the issue is temporarily stalled. Kurtzleben identifies individualistic ideology, weak organized labor, and well-funded business lobbying as the culprits.

If you've been paying attention to the political news in the past couple of years, you know that the U.S. stands virtually alone in not mandating paid leave of any type for its workers.

It's hard to miss; the topic has become a top talking point for Democratic politicians. Hillary Clinton is advocating for stronger paid-leave policies on the campaign trail. In her Monday economic address, Clinton called for paid family leave as a way of helping women stay in the workforce. Sen. Bernie Sanders, her closest rival for the Democratic nomination, has advocated both paid vacation and paid maternity leave on the campaign trail. In addition, some cities and states have started instituting their own sick leave policies.

President Obama likewise brought new attention to paid leave this year as well, when he pointed out in his State of the Union address that the U.S. is the only advanced economy that doesn't mandate paid sick or maternity leave for its workers.

He was right about that—it's true that most American workers are covered by the Family Medical Leave Act, which allows workers up to 12 weeks of leave per year to care for family members. But that leave is unpaid.

Figure 1 shows where the U.S. stands on paid maternity leave in comparison with other countries in the OECD, a group of highly developed economies.

The U.S. is the only one that doesn't mandate paid maternity leave. Likewise, the U.S. is one of nine OECD countries that have no leave policies in place for fathers.

It's not just parental leave, of course—when it comes to vacation, the U.S. is also unique. Figure 2 on page 82 shows combined mandatory vacation days and federal holidays in all OECD nations. All of the U.S. days represented are federal holidays (which are also not guaranteed days off for all workers); the rest of the nations mandate paid vacation days in addition.

It's a similar story on sick days—among high-income countries, the U.S. alone does not mandate sick leave, according to data compiled by the World Policy Forum.

It's not at all new to point this out, but data like these pose a tougher question: How did it get this way? Why is the U.S. so different from the rest of the world in not giving workers paid days off?

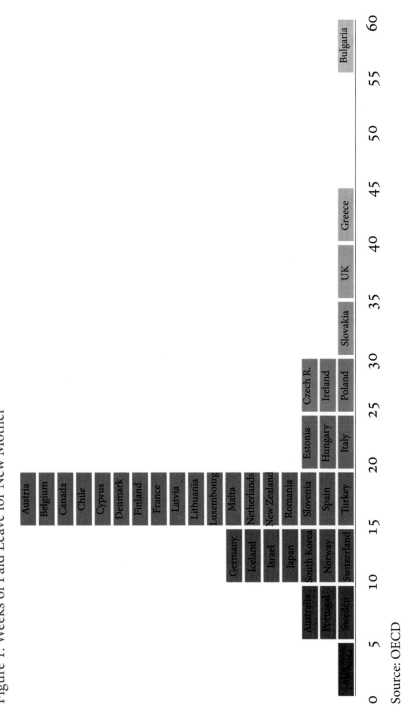

Figure 1: Weeks of Paid Leave for New Mother

Source: OECD

Figure 2: The US Falls Behind in Vacation Days

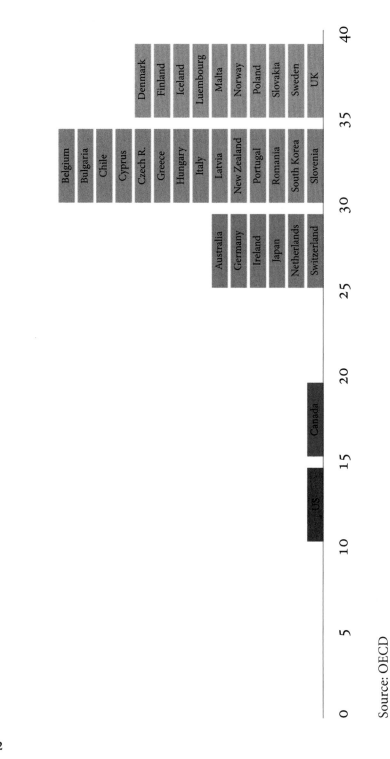

Source: OECD

You could write an entire book about the complicated forces at work here, but a mix of a few big factors has helped set this scene: The aftermath of World War II, business lobbying, a diminished American labor movement, and the American love of individualism and bootstrap-pulling all have combined to help keep the U.S. alone in not giving its workers paid leave.

American Democracy Is Different

One way of thinking about why the U.S. stands alone on paid leave is to zoom way, way out and consider how Americans think about democracy in general—another area where Americans are arguably unique.

Political scientist Seymour Martin Lipset spent much of his career thinking about American exceptionalism—trying to understand what exactly makes the U.S. such a strange creature. Our voting rates are low, but our volunteering rates are high, he pointed out. We're deeply religious. And while some European democracies went in a more socialist direction, the U.S. veered the other way.

For a variety of reasons, Lipset argued, Americans have a different way of thinking about their democracy—the young American democracy was founded with values like individualism and equality of opportunity at its center. And unlike many European democracies, the U.S. has never been a monarchy or a feudal society—that means there's less awareness of class divisions and less deference to the state in the U.S., Lipset writes. He also proposes a similar explanation for how labor parties and trade unions managed to be stronger in other countries but not in the U.S.—where there's less class awareness, there's less likelihood to join unions. (This is just one of many factors he uses to explain U.S. unions' relative weakness, however.)

It's easy to see how that might play out in the realm of paid-leave policies. First of all, with less labor power, there's less support of these sorts of policies. But in addition, when it comes to social class, individualistic, ambitious Americans think of not where they are but where they assume they eventually could be.

"[Lipset's] argument was that Americans identify with the social class that they aspire to rather than the social class that they were in," explains Peter Cappelli, professor of management at the Wharton School at the University of Pennsylvania. "So Americans have a lot of sympathy for small business because American people you would have thought were workers historically thought of themselves as potentially being small-business people."

The result is that Americans tend to have a bit more sympathy for business—after all, when we all own our own shops someday, we won't want our hands tied by any more regulations than absolutely necessary.

How World War II Explains U.S. Maternity Leave

It's not just that America's attitudes differ from the rest of the world's; the gap in parental leave in particular also has its roots in the aftermath of the world wars.

"The European social democracies that emerged after WWII all wanted paid leave policies (some had them earlier) in part because of their concern about replenishing the population," Ruth Milkman, a professor of sociology at CUNY, wrote in an email.

Europe suffered both massive casualties and massive damage to its infrastructure, Milkman explains, and it needed to get more people into the workplace. That meant helping women get into work. Meanwhile, when the U.S. troops came home, it meant less of a need for women in the workplace.

"Here in the U.S., while the war was going on, you had women in jobs in factories and in all kinds of jobs the men had held. But women went home" when the soldiers returned from the war, explains Debra Ness, president of the National Partnership on Women and Families. And with all of those women returning to the home, there was less of a reason to create policies that helped them stay in the workplace.

A Loud Business Voice

One other force opposing paid leave is the business community. Trade groups like the National Federation of Independent Business and chambers of commerce at the state and national levels have repeatedly opposed paid-leave policies. In 2007, one U.S. Chamber of Commerce official said his organization would wage "all-out war" against paid-leave laws.

Businesses are not opposed to paid leave itself; 65 percent of U.S. civilian workers have paid sick leave, and 74 percent have paid vacation, according to the Labor Department. (The numbers are, however, slimmer for paid family leave—only 12 percent of private sector workers have access to that.)

But those in the business community say they're opposed to the government telling businesses how to institute those policies. Paid leave is expensive, they argue, and businesses should all be able to figure it out on their own.

"The challenge with mandates is it is a government one-size-fits-all approach that tries to bring all of these unique workforces and workplaces under this one-size-fits-all approach," says Lisa Horn, spokeswoman at the Society for Human Resource Management, a trade group for HR workers. "It limits workplace flexibility and company innovation in this area."

The U.S.'s campaign finance system helps businesses keep these laws off the books, says one expert.

"Money plays a role in politics in many countries, but the extent to which the amount of dollars [is] spent on campaigns in the United States just dwarfs the amount spent in campaigns elsewhere," says Jody Heymann, dean of the School of Public Health at UCLA. "The ability [to make] very large corporate contributions plays a much more substantial role in our elections than in other countries."

With paid leave a top issue for the two front-running Democratic presidential candidates, conservative groups that oppose paid-leave laws will certainly find themselves fighting this fight in 2016, just as big-spending liberal groups that support paid-leave laws, like unions, will be pushing the cause of inching the U.S. a little bit closer to its international peers in this area.

14

The Women's Rights Movement Still Faces Backlash and Misunderstanding

Dominique Colbert

Dominique Colbert is a hotline crisis services specialist at the Action Alliance. She graduated from Virginia Commonwealth University with a BS in mass communications and a BA in African American studies.

In our final viewpoint, Dominique Colbert surveys a few articles that circulated widely in the aftermath of the historic January 21, 2017, Women's March on Washington that drew three million participants worldwide. Surprisingly, a few women writers seized this moment as an opportunity to denigrate feminism. According to the author, many of these critiques are based on logical fallacies, as well as misunderstandings of feminism's true aim. For example, author Gina Davis overestimates the status of women in America and reiterates the familiar argument that feminism "silences" men, rather than giving voice to unheard women. Such attempts to discredit feminism reverberate via the internet and have an outsized negative impact on progressive goals.

A few weeks ago, history was made. On January 21st, one day after the 2017 Presidential Inauguration, over 3 million people took part in what has been referred to as the largest demonstration

"Dear Daughters of the World: I Did March for You," by Dominique Colbert, Alliance in Action, February 21, 2017. Reprinted with permission from AllianceinAction.org, the project of Virginia Sexual and Domestic Violence Action Alliance.

in U.S. history. The Women's March on Washington, held at the National Mall in Washington, D.C. drew around 500,000 people, while more than 1,000 sister marches took place in all 50 states and in over 32 countries across the globe.

As someone who attended the march, I can attest to the abundance of positive energy spread throughout the day by all in attendance. The feelings of unity and empowerment in one cause was indescribable and unforgettable. Attending was one of the best decisions I have made, and the spark it ignited continue to create positive change has been so rewarding.

Following the march, many news organizations released stories detailing the event's unity, message, and impact. However, anti-feminist articles were also put into high circulation. Most were written by women who claimed to be against the march and feminism altogether. Two such articles were *How the Women's March Reinforced Every Negative Stereotype About Women EVER* and *Dear Daughter: Here's Why I Didn't March For You.* Another article, published prior to the march, *I Am a Female and I Am So Over Feminists* was recirculated heavily. All three articles attempt to disgrace feminism all while showing through their words, their ignorance of the true goal of feminism.

Susan Goldberg, author of *How the Women's March Reinforced Every Negative Stereotype,* makes an effort to vilify the march on the idea that it ignores issues which she sees as more valid. A poster-child for the Fallacy of Relative Privation, Goldberg writes, "America's women have more freedom and dignity than most women in the world." She states that the march should have been for women in other countries who are "working against [their] wills as sex slaves…or [who face] a lifetime of harassment and abuse because [they live] in an Islamic society, or [who are] suffering in silence after having an abortion, or [who are] still suffering the trauma of being tossed away because she was born a girl."

She overlooks the fact that the march *was* worldwide in attendance as well as being centered around the treatment of women worldwide. While some marched across the globe in solidarity with America, some marched for issues more relevant to where they live. Depending on where one lives, the immediate effects of feminism may look different. However, feminist agendas around the world intersect to accomplish the same goal. Oppression is not a contest. One form does not minimize the seriousness of another.

I Am a Female and I Am So Over Feminists is another article that fails to recognize this. Author Gina Davis claims that "Women have never been more respected. Women have more rights in the United States than anywhere else in the world." Ironic, considering for example, that the United States ranks 101st in the world for percentage of women who hold national office. Early in the article, she writes, "God forbid a man has ideas these days," implying that feminists fight to keep men from having and sharing opinions. On the contrary, feminism is a resistance to the erasure of women's voices, not an effort to erase men's.

Mary Ramirez, author of the *Dear Daughter* article chimes in with the same assertion. Ramirez writes that the Women's March was unnecessary because we live in a country where we "already enjoy all the freedoms and rights that men do." She goes on to list off said rights: women can vote, run major companies, or even run for president. It is ironic that in her list of women's freedoms in this country, Ramirez fails to bring up any of the rights women were *actually* marching for at the Women's March. The rights she did list, were, in another ironic twist, fought for by feminists in the past so that we may have them now.

Instead of making valid arguments against any of the issues feminists fight to change, all three articles attempt to discredit the entire feminist movement. *Dear Daughter* describes the marchers as "very loud" women who "screamed" and wore "funny outfits." She goes on to generalize their concerns as "terrible, horrible, no good very bad lies," basing all of her arguments against feminist issues on her altered idea of what feminism actually is. As opposed to paying attention to the marchers' messages of equal rights—equal pay, control of our own bodies, equal treatment of all races, equal opportunities, etc.—they paint their own ideas of what went on at the march and what it meant.

Ironically, *Dear Daughter* and *I Am a Female* conclude with statements that line up with the exact point of feminism: all genders should be treated equally. Davis concludes, saying, "There is no 'dominant' gender... Time to embrace it." Meanwhile, Ramirez states, "...[women are] biologically and physically and emotionally different from men, but that doesn't mean we're less." So congratulations ladies, you too have feminist ideals. Once the time is taken to understand what feminism actually is and what it stands for, a lot more anti-feminist arguments will be dismantled.

Organizations to Contact

The editors have compiled the following list of organizations concerned with the issues debated in this book. The descriptions are derived from materials provided by the organizations. All have publications or information available for interested readers. The list was compiled on the date of publication of the present volume; the information provided here may change. Be aware that many organizations take several weeks or longer to respond to inquiries, so allow as much time as possible.

American Civil Liberties Union (ACLU)
125 Broad Street, 18th Floor
New York, NY 10004
phone: (212) 549-2500
website: http://www.aclu.org

For almost one hundred years, the ACLU has worked to defend and preserve the individual rights and liberties guaranteed by the Constitution and laws of the United States.

Center for Reproductive Rights
199 Water Street
New York, NY 10038
phone: (917) 637-3600
email: info@reprorights.org
website: http://www.reproductiverights.org

For more than twenty years, the Center for Reproductive Rights has used the law to advance reproductive freedom as a fundamental human right that all governments are legally obligated to protect, respect, and fulfill.

Guttmacher Institute
125 Maiden Lane, 7th Floor
New York, NY 10038
phone: (212) 248-1111
email: media@guttmacher.org
website: http://www.guttmacher.org

The Guttmacher Institute is a leading research and policy organization committed to advancing sexual and reproductive health and rights in the United States and globally.

NARAL Pro-Choice America
1156 15th Street NW, Suite 700
Washington, DC 20005
phone: (202) 973-3000
website: http://www.prochoiceamerica.org

The 1.2 million member activists of NARAL Pro-Choice America fight for reproductive freedom for every person in every state. Each day, it organizes and mobilizes to protect that freedom by fighting for access to abortion care, birth control, paid parental leave, and protections from pregnancy discrimination.

National Abortion Federation
1090 Vermont Avenue NW, Suite 1000
Washington, DC 20005
phone: (202) 667-5881
email: naf@prochoice.org
website: http://www.nafcanada.org

The National Abortion Federation (NAF) is a professional association of abortion providers. Members include individuals, private and nonprofit clinics, Planned Parenthood affiliates, women's health centers, physicians' offices, and hospitals that together care for approximately half the women who choose abortion in the United States and Canada each year. Its members also include public hospitals and both public and private clinics in Mexico City and private clinics in Colombia.

National Latina Institute for Reproductive Health

phone: (212) 422-2553
email: HumanResources@latinainstitute.org
website: http://www.latinainstitute.org/en

The National Latina Institute for Reproductive Health (NLIRH) builds Latina power to guarantee the fundamental human right to reproductive health, dignity and justice. It elevates Latina leaders, mobilizes families and communities, transforms the cultural narrative, and catalyzes policy change.

National Network of Abortion Funds

PO Box 170280
Boston, MA 02117
website: http://www. abortionfunds.org

The National Network of Abortion Funds builds power with members to remove financial and logistical barriers to abortion access by centering people who have abortions and organizing at the intersections of racial, economic, and reproductive justice.

National Women's Law Center

11 Dupont Circle NW, # 800
Washington, DC 20036
phone: (202) 588-5180
website: http://www.nwlc.org

The National Women's Law Center has worked for more than forty years to protect and promote equality and opportunity for women and families. It champions policies and laws that help women and girls achieve their potential at every stage of their lives—at school, at work, at home, and in retirement. Its staff are committed advocates who take on the toughest challenges, especially for the most vulnerable women.

Planned Parenthood
123 William Street, 10th Floor
New York, NY 10038
phone: (800) 430-4907
email: info@plannedparenthood.org
website: http://www.plannedparenthood.org

Planned Parenthood is a trusted health care provider, an informed educator, a passionate advocate, and a global partner helping similar organizations around the world. Planned Parenthood delivers vital reproductive health care, sex education, and information to millions of people worldwide.

Women's Global Network for Reproductive Rights
#3 Marunong Street
Barangay Central, Diliman
Quezon City, 1100, Philippines
email: office@wgnrr.org
website: http://wgnrr.org

Women's Global Network for Reproductive Rights is a global network that builds and strengthens movements for sexual and reproductive health and rights (SRHR) and justice. Its work is grounded in the realities of those who most lack economic, social, and political power. Through critical analysis and strategic actions, it connects members and allies, builds knowledge, organizes campaigns, and shares resources. WGNRR works to realize the full sexual and reproductive health and rights of all people, with a particular focus on the most marginalised. It believes that achieving this goal requires transformative social change.

Bibliography

Books

Laura Briggs. *How All Politics Became Reproductive Politics: From Welfare Reform to Foreclosure to Trump* (Reproductive Justice: A New Vision for the 21st Century). Oakland, CA: University of California Press, 2017.

Charles C. Camosy. *Beyond the Abortion Wars: A Way Forward for a New Generation.* Grand Rapids, MI: Wm. B. Eerdmans Publishing Co., 2015.

Barbara Gurr. *Reproductive Justice: The Politics of Health Care for Native American Women.* New Brunswick, NJ: Rutgers University Press, 2014.

Karissa Haugeberg. *Women Against Abortion: Inside the Largest Moral Reform Movement of the Twentieth Century* (Women in American History). Urbana, IL: University of Illinois Press, 2017.

Erica Miller. *Happy Abortions: Our Bodies in the Era of Choice.* London, UK: Zed Books, 2017.

Candida R. Moss and Joel S. Baden. *Bible Nation: The United States of Hobby Lobby.* Princeton, NJ: Princeton University Press, 2017.

Jennifer Nelson. *Women of Color and the Reproductive Rights Movement.* New York, NY: New York University Press, 2003.

Laury Oaks. *Giving Up Baby: Safe Haven Laws, Motherhood, and Reproductive Justice.* New York, NY: New York University Press, 2015.

Willie Parker. *Life's Work: A Moral Argument for Choice.* New York, NY: Atria Books, 2017.

Loretta Ross and Rickie Solinger. *Reproductive Justice: An Introduction* (A New Vision for the 21st Century). Oakland, CA: University of California Press, 2017.

Carol Sanger. *About Abortion: Terminating Pregnancy in Twenty-First-Century America*. Cambridge, MA: Belknap Press, 2017.

Johanna Schoen. *Abortion After Roe: Abortion After Legalization* (Studies in Social Medicine). Chapel Hill, NC: University of North Carolina Press, 2017.

Rickie Solinger. *Reproductive Politics: What Everyone Needs to Know*. New York, NY: Oxford University Press, 2013.

Alisa Von Hagel and Daniela Mansbach. *Reproductive Rights in the Age of Human Rights: Pro-life Politics from Roe to Hobby Lobby*. Basingstoke, UK: Palgrave Macmillan, 2016.

Vicki Oransky Wittenstein. *Reproductive Rights: Who Decides?* Minneapolis, MN: Twenty-First Century Books, 2016.

Periodicals and Internet Sources

Kelly Baden, "How 2017 Could Actually Be a Good Year for the Reproductive Rights Movement," Bustle, January 24, 2017. https://www.bustle.com/articles/201413-how-2017 -could-actually-be-a-good-year-for-the-reproductive -rights-movement.

Priscilla Frank, "A Free, Lady-Led Zine Is Here to School You on Reproductive Rights," Huffington Post, February 23, 2017. www.huffingtonpost.com/entry/reproductive-rights -zine_us_58adab8ee4b04a0b274e93b1.

Amy Howe, "Gorsuch on Abortion, Religion and Reproductive Rights," SCOTUS Blog, March 9, 2017. http://www .scotusblog.com/2017/03/gorsuch-abortion-religion -reproductive-rights.

Olga Khazan, "How Activists Are Protecting Reproductive Rights Under Trump," *Atlantic*, January 25, 2017. https://www.theatlantic.com/health/archive/2017/01/protecting-reproductive-rights-state-by-state/514364.

P. R. Lockhart, "The State of Reproductive Health Legislation in 2017 Is Not Exactly What You Would Expect," *Mother Jones*, April 17, 2017. http://www.motherjones.com/politics/2017/04/guttmacher-report-abortion-restrictions-proactive-legislation-first-quarter-2017.

Amanda Marcotte, "As the GOP Attacks on Birth Control Increase, a New Paper Demonstrates Its Economic Value," Salon, June 7, 2017. http://www.salon.com/2017/06/07/as-gop-attacks-on-birth-control-increase-new-paper-demonstrates-its-economic-value.

Dorothy Roberts, "Reproductive Justice, Not Just Rights," Dissent, Fall 2015. https://www.dissentmagazine.org/article/reproductive-justice-not-just-rights.

Preethi Sundaram, "Caring About Women's Work: Why Sexual and Reproductive Rights Matter," Women Deliver, January 9, 2017. http://womendeliver.org/2017/caring-womens-work-sexual-reproductive-rights-matter.

Heidi Williamson and Jamila Taylor, "The Hyde Amendment Has Perpetuated Inequality in Abortion Access for 40 Years," Center for American Progress, September 29, 2016. https://www.americanprogress.org/issues/women/reports/2016/09/29/145009/the-hyde-amendment-has-perpetuated-inequality-in-abortion-access-for-40-years.

Index